HOW I GREW WITH MY GARDEN

By Priya Vincent

© Copyright 2006 by Priya Vincent
All Rights Reserved

ISBN 978-1-4303-0618-4

DEDICATION

To you.

Deeply felt in

The garden of

My heart.

As the hawk flew,

Like a silky whisper,

Across the dawn

Sky

And with much love to my daughters Emma and Rachael because you were there with me

Grateful thanks to Abha for your wonderfully empathic editing of this book. Thanks to all who have helped and continue to help me in Buddha Garden.

CONTENTS

1. **SEED** – SEARCHING AND FINDING

    The journey to the land called Buddha Garden   page 1

2. **GERMINATION** – GROWING AND LEARNING

    Setting up the vegetable garden   page 25

3. **BECOMING** – CREATION AND DESTRUCTION

    Expanding Buddha Garden into a farm   page 55

4. **QUIESCENCE** – DEPARTURE AND RETURN

    The process of leaving Buddha Garden and the return with new ideas   page 85

5. **REGENERATION** – WEAVING THE WEB BEING WOVEN

    Something new grows from the old   page 113

PART ONE

SEED

SEARCHING AND FINDING

When did it begin? Where did it come from? This deep and unfathomable feeling inside that urges me to connect with the earth and grow food. A passion which has motivated the many experiences and moves I have needed to reach Buddha Garden. This place where, for the last six years, I have engaged with the earth in response to the deepest feelings of my heart.

FIRST BIRTH

Out of the watery mud and reeds
Became I.
Violent skies, sharp Norfolk light
Wide open vistas
Were my first sights
Tempered was I in the cutting
East wind, cold, and
Dazzling sun.

To go back to the point of my first real connection with the earth is to go back to a second birthplace. To the Western Ghats in India, those mountains which stretch like a green backbone down the southwestern slope of the sub-continent. The first time I made the journey I did so with my two daughters, Emma then aged seven and Rachael aged three. We drove up the mountain, the taxi hooting wildly as it hurtled toward the many blind corners of the hair-pin bends while we rolled around in the back. Close to the top of the mountain, and just before we approached the hill station of Kodaikanal, we took a turning and began to drive downwards going five more kilometres along a road of mud and stone only navigable on foot or with a four wheel drive vehicle.

Eventually we came to the place known as 'the Centre', an organic farm with a small Krishnamurthi-type school situated at the bottom of a valley and enclosed by a landscape of stunning beauty. The surrounding hills did not have the superhuman grandeur of the Himalayas, but were what I came to think of as mountains on a human scale. Large enough to feel they were a challenge to scale but with vegetation right to their peaks. I came to see these hills as the living backdrop to my coming to terms with the people, the place, and my own seemingly incomprehensible reasons for being there.

How I Grew With My Garden

We lived in a house with earth walls, small windows with wooden shutters under a roof made of panels that looked like asbestos but were a form of compressed grass. My house was very isolated, its three small adjacent rooms looking east across to the other side of the valley. The sun rising over the opposite mountain woke us on many mornings. Next to the house was a water tank which collected the rain water as it ran off a rock behind the house as well as the roof. This was our water for the bathroom, but the amount was insufficient for anything more than showers and the toilet, so our laundry had to be done in the river.

I came to know that river very well. It ran along the lower part of the valley bisecting the farm and had, for a short distance alongside it, the only level path on the properly. Early each morning, quite soon after sunrise, I walked down to the river to wash all our clothes. This was my most precious time when I could be with myself before spending the rest of the day with other people. Even in the most difficult of times it was a place of tranquility when I got to know the moods of the river in the different seasons.

When we first arrived in August the rains had swollen the river from its dry season trickle to a singing flow that filled the river's banks. There were still many large stones showing through the water on which I could scrub my clothes. Throughout September the rain increased, eventually coming every afternoon and raising the level of the water so that each morning I found more stones submerged and had to find others on which to do my laundering. The monsoon came in October with large clouds rolling up the valley towards us and on many mornings I found myself washing clothes in the rain. Gradually, and then increasingly quickly, the river rose, until towards the end of the monsoon season after a week of continuous rain it was a raging torrent which swept the bridge away.

As I tuned into the river's different manifestations, I found myself becoming exceptionally sensitised to small changes -- both in the surrounding nature and in people. With the increase in the rains, the river water became progressively cloudy and then gritty until at the height of the monsoon it resembled chocolate soup. Only gradually did I realise that this was one of the effects of the greed and rape of the land that was taking place all around me.

Further up the river many people had bought land purely as an investment. To make money quickly they cut down all the trees for their wood, and with no trees to hold the topsoil, it got washed into the river. The plot owners kept the land until the price went up and then sold it. At first this took a few years but during the time I was there prices started to rise very quickly so that sometimes good profits could be made in only a few months. Over the eighteen months I lived there the river was subject to flash floods, presumably as a consequence of this environmental degradation. At each flood the bridge was washed away despite it being built higher than the previous level.

I loved being in a place where there were only natural sounds for most of the time and I realised how rarely I had experienced this closeness to nature. Few vehicles, apart from those of the farm, came along the road which didn't go much farther than where we lived. We were sufficiently removed from other roads for the noise of vehicles to be heard only rarely.

From a practical point of view, however, the Centre was a difficult place to live. There was no electricity from the grid and although we had a solar system it was somewhat temperamental and seemed to need an inordinate amount of attention to make it work properly. With care we could run our laptop computers but during the monsoon, when there was little sun, we often had light for only an hour or so in the evenings. A lot of things that would normally be done with the help of electricity were done entirely by hand. This included the daily grinding of the rice and dal to make breakfasts of dosai (a sort of pancake) and idli (a kind of steamed rice cake made with the same mixture), to all the carpentry and building work. The latter was particularly difficult as all the building materials such as bags of cement and granite pillars had to be brought in by lorries which could not always make it all the way down to the farm. Even if they did get that far, the materials then had to be carried to the building site on the top of someone's head. Even the wheelbarrow could not be used on some of the paths. As a result building or making furniture took a very long time.

The houses were spread out all over the farm so everyone had a lot of walking to do in the course of their normal daily tasks. Each morning I walked to the river to do my laundry after which I went to the communal kitchen to eat breakfast, and then proceeded on to the school where I used to teach. It was in the school that I started to do some practical work on the land in the so-called 'farm class'. It was part of the ethos of the school that we all participated in growing and preparing food as well as in cleaning and otherwise looking after the school buildings. The parents of the village children who attended the school often could not see the point of this. In their view we were giving their children an education in the English medium that would surely enable them to do more than the same poorly paid and low status work on the land that they were doing. So what was the point of this class? We spent many hours explaining that our concept of education focused on more than just passing exams. It was also about learning how to look after ourselves by growing our food, making clothes, caring for the school building as well as trying to live in harmony with ourselves, each other, and the earth. I enjoyed doing the farm class and learnt with the children about how to grow food in this new environment. At that time it was my only real contact with the farm because teaching in the school was all-consuming and somewhat divorced from the professional farming activities.

There was only a small group of people at the Centre but the tensions were manifold, most of which were unexpressed. Without my partner -- who was finishing off a three-year teaching contract in Africa -- I felt very lonely. We had planned that he would come to live in the Centre with me when his contract was finished, but within the first ten minutes of arriving for the Christmas holiday it was clear that this was not to be. He did not like the difficult and basic lifestyle and what was more important, felt totally at odds with the ideas of Malcom who had set up the Centre and who was still the prime mover for most of what happened there. I could see the problems and feel the many tensions, and yet, despite everything I wanted to stay. There seemed to be something important here for me, although what it was I had no idea.

Being aware of the beauty around me, and being conscious of the river's energy and the way the earth absorbed my negativity gave me an inkling of why I continued stay. So often I would find myself feeling horribly miserable, only to feel it drain away through the soles of my feet as I walked and worked on the land. Being there I was so close to those earth energies that it washard to feel when the skin between myself and the outside was measured in bricks and mortar, and where my feet were insulated from the earth by tarmac and the noise of machines. The beauty and the feelings for nature, however, did not seem to make up for the isolation and loneliness I felt and the lack of fellow feeling for most of the other people with whom I worked. I think it was the earth that held me there although at the time I felt as if I were going mad as I couldn't think of a single rational reason as to why I should stay in this place. .

Yet for most of those first months I was not really engaged with the earth. I was in nature but not of nature, not engaged with the earth or aligned with its energies. This did not begin to happen until after we had visited an organic farm belonging to Narayan Reddy in Bangalore which we did as part of a school excursion. For many of the children it was their first experience outside their immediate geographical area, and most of them had never before travelled on a train.

******

We only stayed for two days but almost immediately as we looked around the farm and helped with the work, I felt in harmony, not only with Narayan Reddy's ideas about organic farming, but also about living lightly and in accord with the earth. His ideas about this were based on the best parts of the Indian agricultural tradition, but he also tried to take advantage of what he considered were appropriate technological advances. In his house, for example, he had a beautiful television set but no chairs as he felt these were unnecessary in the Indian context.

After my experience there I was fired with enthusiasm to try growing more for ourselves. It had always seemed impractical to me that we didn't grow more of our own vegetables, but this was partly because of how the farm manager worked. He preferred growing large quantities for the market and found it difficult to grow small amounts regularly for home use. I began by making my own vegetable garden where I would work before breakfast and in the evenings after school until it got dark. I learnt so much in that garden although the quantities of vegetables that I was able to grow were minute. The most difficult thing was to be aware of all the different factors such as the weather and the soil, in addition to the water requirements and knowing when to plant the right plants at the right time to take advantage of them. I found that going out in the morning to do the physical work and then eating something grown on the farm for a meal was deeply satisfying.

Later, I also looked after the land around my house which consisted of some extremely neglected coffee bushes. Every morning I would go and slash away at the lantana which, like blackberries, entwined itself lovingly around all the plants. This was another way of working on the land that needed more long-term thought. Before coffee bushes would grow shade trees had to be planted, then the bushes had to be planted the correct distance apart as they would be in there for many years. Do it wrong, as had happened in one part of the farm where they were planted too close, and there was little that could be done without starting completely all over again.

In doing this work I began to have the first hints of how it might put me in touch with something which I wanted to understand and feel more profoundly. Giving birth had brought me into contact with powerful energies of creative life and this work on the earth seemed to be doing the same thing in a different way. I felt that living this close to nature and being engaged with it to grow food gave me access both to the cycles of the earth and the cycles of living within myself. That it helped me touch a source of life energy. I also felt very strongly that in trying to heal the land I was also in some way healing myself. Practically it helped me over a lot of psychological problems as well as building up my body after suffering from typhoid. Somewhere I felt there would be healing on a more intense level but at that time how this could happen was very unclear. I felt like an anchorite who in helping to heal one little patch of the earth was helping to heal the whole earth for everyone. I felt I was laying the groundwork for something but didn't know what it was.

One of the things that I missed in this place, however, was any sense of community. Malcom had invested a lot of his money in the Centre and he, despite his protestations to the contrary, dominated everything that was done there – from farming to school activities. He had an Indian wife who seemed much less enthusiastic about the group living he envisaged. I missed my partner greatly and felt very little emotional warmth in the day-to-day work. I used a number of strategies to deal with this, one of them being to work very hard and to get my emotional satisfaction from work rather than from my relationships. In effect I put the emotional side of myself to sleep in order to stay there.

In general when there was a difficult emotional situation, and I experienced many, it tended to be smoothed over rather than openly confronted and transformed. Eventually this happened once too often when I was involved in a tense and volatile situation where it was expected that I would carry on as if nothing had happened. I could not see the point of living in such a way which I felt was fundamentally dishonest, especially in a place that purported to be a 'spiritual community' with a 'new way of being'. I felt strongly that it was time to leave and in the course of a few hours I had made my decision to go and left.

Home is where the heart is
My heart is not here.

For a long time afterwards I grieved for the shattering of this dream and for having to leave this land that I had loved. I missed not only the beauty of the place but also my engagement with the land which I felt was leading me to a different way of being that was important to reveal to myself and others. I do not know, though, how long I could have stayed there with the emotional side of myself dormant. Healing is to become whole and I do not think this would have been possible in this place where the only way to be there was to deny an important part of myself.

We all went to live with my partner in the nearby school in which he was teaching. Despite the negative aspects of this experience I felt more than ever that I wanted to not only live close to nature, but also engage with the land. That I wanted to live in a place with a spiritual focus became an absolute certainity.

******

'Auroville wants to be a universal town where men and women of all countries are able to live in peace and progressive harmony, above all creeds, all politics and all nationalities. The Purpose of Auroville is to realise human unity.'

Inspired by the work of the Indian spiritual visionary Sri Aurobindo, Auroville was founded in 1968 by his spiritual collaborator known as the Mother. It was set up as a collective experiment to create a bridgehead for a new consciousness which was seeking to manifest itself in the world. The name 'Auroville' was given in homage to Sri Aurobindo, while also having the most appropriate meaning, 'City of Dawn'.

I first came to Auroville with a group of students from the school where my partner was teaching. His neighbour, Pippa, was in charge of the excursion and thought with my interest in spiritual communities I might be interested in seeing what was going on. There was room on the bus and in the youth hostel where they were going to stay although, it being February and the height of the guest season, Pippa thought it most unlikely I would find somewhere to stay in Auroville. I found, however, that the largest and busiest guest house had a spare room for three days and with that, a way seemed to open into Auroville. While staying there I was told by an Aurovilian that if I was thinking of coming to Auroville I would find it difficult to find somewhere to live and work. Yet during my short stay I not only found work in one of the schools, but also somewhere to live. The earth didn't move and the bells didn't ring; I didn't feel that ecstatic certainty of 'this is it. This is what I have been searching for.' Rather it felt as if things had arranged themselves so that the way opened and the next obvious step was to move to Auroville.

Two weeks later this was what I did, coming in a large van with Emma and Rachael and all our belongings packed in boxes.

It was all a far cry from the pristine beauty and silence of the Valley. We lived in a large community called New Creation that was busy and noisy with a kindergarten, secondary school (where I worked) as well as several businesses or 'units' as they are known in Auroville. One of these was a taxi service with taxis that were parked outside my room. At all hours of the day and night the smell and noise of their engines was very evident. The worst thing for me was all the rubbish spread over the field outside the gate which I had to pass every time I entered or left the community. It had been dumped there from nearby Pondicherry, this being the traditional way in which the town supported the food growing of the surrounding country. When the waste was all organic it worked well as it provided compost for the fields. With modern unsorted waste, however, it looked and smelt terrible. I wondered why I was here every time I went through the gate. Every time I asked the universe whether this was my place, I seemed to hear a very resounding 'YES'. Considering the circumstances I felt this couldn't just be me dreaming.

Compared with the Valley there was a plethora of different things that I could do and many more people with whom I could interact. In those first weeks I was subject to many tempting offers – too many as I found it impossible to make up my mind what to do. Obviously the work had to fit in with Emma and Rachael (which was not usually too difficult as work hours were, by contrast with the Valley, very short) but I also wanted to feel a rightness about it for myself. How could I choose? In the end I decided I should choose work that would enable me to manifest the highest expression of myself, but exactly what that was took me many years to find out. I felt strongly to work on the land in a community, but this didn't seem possible in the present situation.

Having just come from working in a school that was very connected with the land and having had a 'farm garden' with a 'farm class,' I very much wanted to continue that as part of my teaching at New Creation school. Things were very different however. Whereas at the Centre the farm was seen as integral with the school, in New Creation, doing work in the vegetable garden was seen as a not very popular optional extra. The children at this school came because they wanted – or their parents wanted them – to do something 'better' than farming.

Despite this I decided that I would try to start a garden in the community. There was little enthusiasm but I started a small garden on a piece of land just outside my house. I was looked at with some bemusement by the employed gardeners who had their own way of doing things and made it quite clear that they didn't think this was suitable work for a white woman.

The first thing I did was to try and build a compost heap as I could see there was no lack of organic material although it was not being handled very well. It was flung into a pit with the rest of the rubbish which from time-to-time would be burnt, making a huge pall of acrid smoke. With some difficulty I managed to get the kitchen to separate the organic and non-organic rubbish and used the organic rubbish to make my first compost heap, mixing it with dung from the community cows.

Unfortunately, I had not taken into account the many dogs who came in their droves from the nearby village and in a very short space of time managed to dismantle the compost heap completely. I built a wire cage around the next heap to keep the dogs out but I found that unless I used very strong and expensive wire they would wreck it completely. Even when I found a wire strong enough to keep them out they were extremely persistent. They worked at taking the top off or hung around watching and waiting until someone didn't put the lid on properly so that they could move the top to get into the food.

I arrived in Auroville in February and started the garden in March which is quite the wrong time of year as it is just before the very hot season when there is no rain. The soil was very poor and I had no idea what to grow. I tried growing radish which had grown so rampantly in the Centre but will only grow in Auroville when the night temperature falls below 25C which doesn't happen until September/October and only lasts for a few months.

Water was much more of a problem than in the mountains where there was only one three-month period when it did not rain. I soon came to realise that in Auroville watering was a daily time-consuming job unless I used drippers or sprinklers. At this time I knew no one who knew anything about this, so I continued to use a hose, grabbing it first thing in the morning before the gardeners came to work.

With all the dogs and other difficulties it was no surprise when the garden could hardly get going. I planted seeds, but those that came up had not only the heat to contend with but dogs, insects, and other pests. They barely managed to grow let alone produce anything. I suppose I could have put a fence around it but that would have cost a lot of money and it was not clear whether the garden was really wanted or needed. As I worked in it I was conscious all the time that I was the only one really interested and that if the land were needed for building then there would be no question that the garden would have to go.

To my surprise, the dynamics of the New Creation community were similar to the ones I had experienced at the Centre, despite the larger number and diversity of people involved. There was one person who had set up the community and who dominated the activities despite his protestations to the contrary. There seemed to be no commitment towards transforming difficult situations between people, and things were either ignored or smoothed over just as they had been in the Centre. I seemed to be dealing with exactly the same problems as before and couldn't understand why this should be so. Had I not learnt the lessons at the Valley? If I had, why should I be confronted with exactly the same experience again? It is only looking back on it that I can see that during the second experience I got a deeper understanding of what was going on and could envision more creative ways of dealing with it. Sometimes we need the same lesson twice.

******

Having seen the limitations of the small group in the Valley, I hoped that within the very much larger community of Auroville, with its several settlements, there would be a greater possibility of living within a community. I hoped that I would be able to find one that was focused on working on the land. As well as providing both practical and emotional support I felt that the right place could also be a potent crucible for my spiritual growth. Having decided to stay in Auroville I started looking around for somewhere more in tune with my thinking.

Such a place was difficult to find. So many so-called communal settlements were started by one person who was the prime mover and continued to play a pivotal part in the group. There were very few places where people ate or worked together or where there were community processes which facilitated individual growth and group cohesion. The nearby community/settlement of Aspiration seemed to have at least some of the characteristics of a community – the residents all ate together twice a day with everyone taking turns to cook. As far as I knew there was nowhere else in Auroville where this was happening. There appeared to be no clear way of becoming a community member, but by dint of going there as a guest and participating in what community life there was, we were eventually accepted for a trial period of three months.

By this time we had become Newcomers, the (then) one-year orientation period necessary before becoming Aurovilians. We moved into the Newcomer accommodation, and with both children being able to go to Auroville schools they were ecstatic. By this time I had stopped working in the New Creation NC School and, instead, was doing various sorts of work in the Health Centre where I kept my computer and books and did my writing.

Despite being part of a large group of people and having a limited sort of community life I felt very lonely in Aspiration. We had community meetings every now and then but the place seemed very fractured. There were some groups of people who seemed to have more influence about what went on than others, but I was not a member of any of them and unlikely to be so. I did not feel close to many people in the community and did not feel much of a community spirit. I seemed to be the only one there completely on my own although, of course, I was looking after Emma and Rachael.

My ambivalent feelings about the community were stimulated by the death of one of the community members soon after I arrived. I can't remember her name now, but remember seeing her once or twice, the last time being when I was sitting with another community member just outside the dining room. This wraith-like woman flitted in front of us on her way to the kitchen to get some milk. 'Whose that?' I asked my companion, but she was also new to the community and had never seen her before. The woman looked emaciated, but being a newcomer both to Auroville and the community, I didn't feel to take it any further. Sitting there I got the first feelings of 'its not my problem therefore I don't have any responsibility to do anything,' or 'I've got enough on my plate as it is without taking on more.' After just a few months in Auroville, it seemed that the rampant individualism of the place was slowly starting to seep into my being even though I had chosen to live in a place that was more of a community than most places in Auroville.

A week later I heard that she had been found unconscious in her bathroom – quite by chance - when someone went to visit her. It seemed that for some years she had suffered from anorexia and from time-to-time had had to be 'rescued' by the community who jollied her along to participate sometimes in meals and other activities. This time, because it was summer and there were fewer people around, it hadn't happened and she had starved herself to the point of collapse. She was taken to the local hospital where soon after she died.
Although the community was to some degree shaken by her death there was little real feeling expressed, as far as I could see. Surely there was something wrong within a community where this could be allowed to take place? The

overall feeling seemed to be, however, that when people are allowed their individual freedom then sometimes things like this would happen. We all had to take individual responsibility for our spiritual growth, and in this case certain distortions within had led to her death. In the past her greatest excesses had been picked up before they were fatal, but this time unfortunately not. Perhaps it was part of the greater plan that she should die now. From time to time these things happen and the general feeling was that there was little that could be done to avoid such events.

******

My greatest friend at this time was Angelique who came to stay as a guest in the room next to mine. The first time I saw her she was walking along the path beautifully dressed in a sophisticated style that made me think we couldn't possibly have anything in common. I couldn't have been more wrong. Angelique had come with her daughter and two sons to Auroville, after a difficult year when she had been sick and cured herself of cancer by natural methods. She had come to see if Auroville was the place where she would like to live. Her eldest son soon returned to their home in Europe and her daughter, who was depressed in the beginning, gradually got better in the following six months. Angelique was a healer and soon started work and quickly built up a clientele. We spent a long time talking to each other about our thoughts about Auroville and our reactions to community events which she helped me to see in a deeper and more profound way, rather than just the presenting problems that they seemed to be.

Ever since I had been in Auroville I continued to be in close contact with my partner. We went to see him in Kodaikanal at regular intervals and we wrote to each other every day. We were conscious that although we lived apart we were still very connected. One Sunday morning it came as a terrible shock to hear that he had been assaulted the previous night and had lain unconscious in his house for fourteen hours before being found by a neighbour and taken to hospital. Immediately we dropped everything and went to be with him. After a week he had recovered enough to be brought back to Aspiration where I could look after him. Ten days later he unexpectedly, and very suddenly, died.

For a moment in time
You are here.

In a moment of time
You go.

At the next moment
You have left.

Leaving an empty
Loneliness

Unbearably long.

The community, apart from a few notable individuals, was extremely unhelpful. Many felt that he should not be buried in Auroville because he was not Aurovilian. Just hours before we were due to bury him that evening in a nearby forest, there was a community meeting to decide whether this should happen or not. Punch drunk with grief I went through everything as if in a painful dream from which I felt I would never emerge.

In the weeks and months that followed, Angelique generously supported and shared her depths with me. Her husband had died soon after the birth of her youngest son and as a result she had much empathy and a resilient love. Ever since then, my partner's death has reverberated both within and without in different ways. Working on the land has been an important part of the healing process for me.

Despite, or maybe because of, the community tensions and the grief, I was keen to start another garden. I still felt that somehow I wanted to engage with the earth as it felt as if something was missing when my days did not include some working on the land. In one of the meetings I asked if I could start a garden and got the usual Aurovilian reply 'if that's what you want to do then you can' although no one else was very interested, wanted to help, or gave me any encouragement. Eventually another Newcomer came to help from time-to-time although her ideas about growing food were somewhat esoteric and she preferred to sit and talk to the plants rather than do the digging. We seemed to muddle along together rather well.

Once again this garden was at the back of where I was living as I had already realized how difficult it was if I did not live close to the land on which I was working. I needed to be close so that I could keep an eye on and tune in to what was going on there. I made so many mistakes but the worst one was that it was in the wrong place. I made the garden there because I had been told the soil would be good. Someone else had made several compost heaps in the same place. Unfortunately, the conditions for making compost were not the right conditions for making a garden. Being shady and damp, it was ideal for making compost, but for a vegetable garden it was too shady with the result that the plants grew long and leggy in an attempt to reach the light.

I had, however, chosen the right time of year for starting a garden. It was just after the start of the summer monsoon which brings the first rains after the very hot months of the summer. Again there was no irrigation system and no nearby tap so watering it every day was a difficult and tedious task. In this community there were two gardeners who did most of the physical work. My making a garden was seen by them as most peculiar and something of an imposition into their world which they had carved out for themselves. The only thing that anyone else in the community did in the garden was to water it when the pump was switched on very early in the morning. Probably the only reason that the gardeners didn't do this job was because they didn't come in at that early hour. Perhaps they felt intimidated at this white woman doing what they considered was unsuitable work. Perhaps they felt I was taking their job away. Whatever it was, they would not share with me anything about what I should grow or how I should grow it. So once again I struggled away on my own although this time the plants did grow and, despite it being too shady, looked like they might even produce something.

Gardening seemed to evoke all my feelings of loneliness and about being in a place where there was neither the will nor the consciousness to work together on anything. Everyone all in their own little bubbles and fearful of anyone who might disturb the life that they had made for themselves. I could not understand where such a way of being came from or what I could do about it. I frequently wondered whether I had made a mistake in coming to Auroville, but the children were very happy both in Aspiration and in their school. I did not feel to disturb this, but it was not the only reason that I stayed. I once asked the universe 'is this my place?' and the next day, as I was walking up the road to the Health Centre I met most of the people that I knew in Auroville, most of whom greeted me with particular warmth. I took this as a sign that I should stay.

One morning I went to work in the garden to find that it had disappeared. I couldn't believe my eyes! Only yesterday the garden had been covered with plants and now there was none. So I looked around and found that the garden had been moved, lock stock and barrel to another part of the community. In many ways it was a better place with more available water and more open to the sun. The gardeners told me that they had, at the request of some members of the community, moved all my plants to this new location.

When I remonstrated about this in a regular meeting, to which I had to get a special dispensation to attend as I was still a Newcomer, no one would take me seriously. I was told that the decision had been made by the community to move the garden to the new location and there wasn't anything I could do about it as it was a 'collective' decision. As my voice rose in the meeting I realized that I was feeling as I did when a young child, when my point of view would not be acknowledged because it was inconvenient for my parents to do so. And the more my voice rose – I had learnt by then it was no use shouting as it turned everyone off completely – I watched the eyes lose focus and the expressions get more stony as they ignored and refused to acknowledge my distress at the way I had been treated.

I stopped gardening and was sick for a month.

******

In this community it seemed that there was little discussion about the things that really mattered, especially when this involved the expression of feelings about what was going on. Unsigned notes would appear on the notice board about what someone thought should be done about a perceived problem. More unsigned notes would be put up in response. I felt strongly that this was no way to be in a community and one day said so to a group of people reading the latest postings on the notice board. I was told not to get excited and not to shout, but I wanted to shout; I felt strongly about this and shouting seemed the only way to make people listen. But of course they were right and shouting doesn't automatically ensure a perceptive listening. There was a very strong ethos that one did not show one's feelings. It wasn't part of the perceived spiritual ideals which were to display an equanimity unsullied by feelings and emotions. Once again it seemed I was in a place where things were smoothed over, this time in the name of spiritual ideals, so that opportunities for internal and external confrontation and transformation remained unavailable.

At the end of our three-month trial period no one told me that they wanted us to leave, but neither would anyone say that we could stay. It was no wonder that I felt as if I were nowhere. Eventually in a community meeting I was told that we didn't fit into the community. They studiously avoided my eyes as they talked to me about it. By this time I knew that there wasn't a real group energy here and that the place had a fractured quality. Despite the overt things like eating together there was no real community. It was like an empty vessel.

I felt rejected despite seeing that this was not the right place for us and that we should move.

******

While in Aspiration I had continued seeing friends in New Creation and was eventually able to make my peace with the place and the people and to be realistic about what was possible there. As I was in the process of working out what to do about leaving Aspiration a house became available in New Creation Field at the back of New Creation. I decided to take it. I did not want to stay any longer than necessary in a place where I did not feel welcome.

Moving into the new house in New Creation Field was one of the most difficult things I have ever had to do. Although I had got used to moving around on my own with the children, to move the week before Christmas and somehow create a special Christmas atmosphere when I felt such grief and loss – when we all felt such grief and loss – was very difficult indeed. With Emma and Rachael's help I somehow managed to do it. In this new house it was for the first time that I had all my things together and a proper work room in which to write. Here I wrote my third book in the privacy of my own creative space. Here I began to think more seriously about my writing and how I should fit this in with the life I was living in Auroville.

I found it ironic that I, who so much wanted to live in community, had ended up living the conventional life of a single mother with all the normal isolation, extra work and responsibilities that this entails. Every morning I took the children to the bus stop to catch the school bus and shopped and prepared meals, doing all the things I would be doing in the same way if I were living anywhere else. I knew that in some ways I needed this break after the tumultuous events of the previous year, but it didn't stop me wondering. If I was going to live such a predictable life, why I was bothering to stay in Auroville? Surely I could live a similar and more comfortable life elsewhere.

There was the front garden to plant, however, and by this time I had a much better idea about the best kind of trees and shrubs to grow. About what grew easily, preferably without too much water, as I was beginning to learn about the water problems of the area. I had also learnt the hard way what a trial it was to have to regularly water plants with a hose. This satisfied my need to work with the earth for a while but soon I felt that I would like to try growing food again. So once again I found another piece of land, earmarked for building but not for several years. It was unfortunately some way from the house and although I built a store room and a strong fence around, with my not being there for so much of the day, it was only partially effective. Somehow the cows seemed to be able to get in.

I joined up with the Child-to-Child health program at the Health Centre which was promoting the setting up of vegetable gardens in the villages. As a result I learnt a lot of very practical information not only about what would grow but how to grow it. From time-to-time I also had help from the children on the program, and also received some lessons from an expert about how to make compost in this type of climate. Regretfully, the watering continued to be a problem as I still did not know about drippers and sprinklers and where to get them or even if they were available.

In the months following my partner's death, the healing qualities of this work were very evident. Many was the time that I went out feeling depressed and after an hour or two's digging and weeding, felt much better. This time many of the seeds germinated and grew into plants and I also managed to obtain some plants of tomato and spinach. We had problems with pests, but despite this we did, intermittently, get vegetables that we could eat. The produce that we grew seemed, in this garden at least, less important than the huge amount I learnt and the healing I received. I also knew that with its sandy soil, this plot would require several seasons work on it to become really productive and that it would probably be needed for building before that would happen. That I had been able to do this work and be on this land, for even a short while, was for me at this time, enough.

******

Becoming more serious about wanting to farm, I made contact with and started to attend farm group meetings. The Farm Group is an association of Aurovilian farmers who meet twice a month to support each other and discuss various issues related to the farms. I was surprised when I went to the first meeting that here was a group of people most of whom I had not seen before. By participating in their discussions I began to understand the issues that needed to be addressed as well as seeing what I would need to do if I were going to set up and run a farm. I become more and more convinced that this was what I wanted to do and started actively looking for a place to do it.

******

The creation of the new community of Adventure started with the opportunity to take over a piece of land in the green belt which had been recently purchased by Auroville. It was a large piece of land – 40 acres – which it seemed would be best planted as a forest but with room for farming as well. I cannot remember quite how I got to know about the available land or how the group who wanted to move there came together, but gradually through various means a group began to coalesce and meet regularly in my house in New Creation. It seemed that at last the land and the people were coming together in a way that I had wanted them to do for so long. Here was the community I wanted so much. Here was the place where we could work together on the land to both heal the land by planting trees, and grow food for the community.

> *'I want to live in a way that I can feel nature's heart beat which I think means living with less of a skin between myself and nature. It's not just a matter of living in a beautiful place but living simply in natural materials and working closely on the land in tune with the greater rhythms of the earth.'*

With the possibility of this new community I felt that all I deeply wanted was going to be manifest.

As a group we were very inexperienced both in working on the land and living in Auroville. Only two of the original seven people had a place to stay in Auroville, so for most of the group finding a place to live was an important reason for wanting to join in. As we were going to live in the green belt we knew that we would have to abide by green belt guidelines and use renewable energy sources – such as windmills for pumping water and solar energy for lights – and in every possible way try to live lightly on the land. This excluded several people who wanted to live 'in nature' but wanted all modern conveniences as well. Many people came because they could build a cheap house, which they were unable to do elsewhere in Auroville, but they were not particularly interested in working on the land. We began meeting regularly and as well as deciding who should be part of the group. We also had to plan how we intended to develop the land and submit these ideas to various groups in Auroville for approval.

Looking back, I felt that we did at the time come to a shared view on what we wanted to do although I think the subsequent problems we experienced showed that this did not go very deep. With our inexperience both in starting a new settlement, and working on the land, we tended, being relatively new to Auroville, to accept and go along with anything that anyone said they wanted to do, provided it seemed in accord with the very broad ideas for development that we had drawn up. I said that I wanted to create a farm and this was accepted but it was only later, when we were on the land and I was trying to do the work, that some members of the group felt that I was doing things that were unacceptable.

In the beginning – our honeymoon period – things went very smoothly. There was a lot of work to do, most of it new to us, in terms of getting a well dug and building the necessary infrastructure of communal kitchen and store room. We worked together very harmoniously and gradually we began to see the place taking shape. I moved to the land very early on with Dirk who was then my lover and for some time lived with him in a very basic capsule with an earth toilet and bathroom consisting of a hose connection to the water source. Rachael came with me and lived in a tent, but Emma preferred to stay in the relative comfort of our New Creation house and didn't want to leave until a 'proper bathroom' had been built.

It was during this period that my Mother died, an event that reactivated all the grief I still felt about the death of my partner. Once again the work on the land and living close to natural rhythms enabled me to cope with these painful feelings. Eventually the infrastructure was finished and everyone could move in and be together. I had very high hopes and began the practical work of creating a farm and growing food.

******

It was in Adventure that I grew my first serious amounts of vegetables – enough to sometimes send some either to the newly opened Solar Kitchen or to Pour Tous, the Auroville distribution center. I felt such a deep satisfaction when I took the vegetables I had grown to these places, even although it was obvious that I still had a long way to go and a lot to learn.

Since it had been agreed that there was to be a farm and that I was to run it, I went ahead and did whatever I thought was necessary, often with Dirk's help, although his real interest was in forestry and planting trees. I began by putting up fences around the vegetable gardens to keep out our dogs as well as the cows and goats that still wandered onto the land. This was perceived by some members of the community as taking the land for myself and since this went counter to the accepted idea that the land was to be held in common this was deemed objectionable. There was also a lot of disagreement over whether we should have animals or not. I felt that given the soil and climate conditions it would be very difficult indeed to farm without animals as their dung is needed to improve the soil. I was wary of taking on cows but built a chicken house and got some chickens to the consternation of some community members who thought it was exploiting animals to keep them either for milk or eggs.

At the same time there were other tensions in the community relating to the community processes we had agreed to. We had decided to have communal meals but then one family said that they wanted to have their own kitchen. We had agreed to have work and sharing meetings but not everyone wanted to participate. Not everyone in the community actually wanted it to be very communal. Things disintegrated badly and great rifts appeared between everyone, especially when I found myself at the center of disagreement between Dirk and the rest of the community. Looking back I know that I could probably have kept the group together if I had acted differently, but this I think would have made the group cohesion dependent on me instead of being something that grew from each of the participants. I realized I was tired of being a go between linking Dirk and everyone else in the community.

Eventually it became clear to me that I could not stay. The ideology concerning how the group wanted to be on the land hindered me from creating a farm in the way that I thought was most appropriate. I did not feel comfortable with the community who were unwilling to support what I wanted to do. My actions had led to a lot of mistrust and the feeling that I was probably more committed to Dirk than to the community. Increasingly I felt more and more disharmonious as the community processes, which I felt had less and less relevance for me, seemed to take precedence over everything else.

Obviously it was time to leave.

******

Dirk and I decided we would go somewhere else together, and eventually we moved to start Siddhartha Forest on another smaller piece of recently acquired land. Once again we found ourselves drilling wells and building and planting a forest. I knew when I moved there that the land was not good enough to farm but I needed a place to be quiet and to heal the grief of that first community not working. How I missed the land of Adventure. I had worked on it for such a short time yet it broke my heart to leave.

In the new community I once again had a vegetable garden, but this time just for ourselves, which again provided me with more experience. I loved to go out there in the evenings and see what there was to cook for our evening meal. It was during this time that grief became my constant companion – as if the grief of leaving the last community compounded the grief of losing my partner and my mother. For a long time I was badly depressed and anorexic. The garden became a haven and growing things a therapy. Several times I went into the garden feeling so depressed I did not think I could survive the next few minutes. Several times, feeling like this, I saw the plants move towards me to give me their healing energy.

Here, over a period of time, I thought a lot about the lessons there had been for me in the Adventure experience. It seemed that to create a real community more was needed than just the intention to do so. It required not only a shared vision, but also a shared agreement as to how that vision was to be made manifest. In Adventure, Dirk and I had shared neither very deeply and it was therefore best that we left creating a space for those to come who did share the vision better. I often wondered if there was a community where I could be, especially when I became more serious about my creative activities. I started to paint, as well as write, and needing a lot of time alone to do this I wondered if this could ever be incorporated in a close community. Obviously it would depend on the community and would perhaps be something that grew spontaneously rather than intentionally. For the time being, at least, I decided, I would work alone and try to follow my deepest passions which still seemed to lead me towards working with the earth to grow food.

I was by this time just a small step away from Buddha Garden.

PART TWO

GERMINATION

GROWTH AND LEARNING

I find it hard to write about the decision to move from Siddhartha Forest to Buddha Garden without it sounding as if it were a linear thought process with one thing leading logically on to another. In fact it was more of a configuration of internal and external things that, in coming together pointed to this move as being the next step for me. There was a certain logic to the process but this could only be seen when looking back – at the time it felt much more chaotic. The movements are difficult to summarise. They included the need I felt to leave Siddhartha Forest, which was very much Dirk's place with nowhere to create a farm and the pull I felt towards Siddhartha Farm where Herbert, who ran the farm, had spare land that I could use.

You should leave
But slowly
And look around
As you go.

Look back with love and thankfulness
Look forward with hope

See all around.

The land that was to become Buddha Garden was part of Siddhartha Farm, our nearest Aurovilian neighbour, which I had been visiting almost daily for some months to get milk. I had never seen it as the site of a possible vegetable garden, much less move there, until a chance remark to Herbert (the farm manager) that I might be looking for a place for a vegetable garden. He jokingly said he had just the place and pointed to the land over which I had just walked to come and see him. As I went back that night I saw the land with new eyes and began to think - yes, maybe I could have a vegetable garden here.

The plot, of about an acre and a half, had been part of Siddhartha Farm for some years but Herbert had been too busy to do anything with it. It was quite close to the farm well and was just the right size for me to both build somewhere to live and have a vegetable garden. It had obviously once been used for growing crops as the bunds (earth banks) around the original three small fields were still very evident. It was covered with spindly, miserable - looking eucalyptus trees and I had the sense of the land being under continual pressure from the herds of goats and cows that roamed across it eating anything that seemed the least bit edible.

Dirk was upset that I wanted to leave, particularly as he felt that with Siddhartha Farm being just next door, I should be able to create and work on a farm and continue living in Siddhartha Forest. I knew this wouldn't work for me (although it works for some farmers in Auroville) and that if I was going to grow food then I would have to live on the land where I was doing it. Only by living on the land would I be able to feel its vibration as well as keep in touch with all the large and small practical details that needed taking care of, often outside normal working hours.

In wanting to create a vegetable garden, however, I was aware that I wanted to do more than just grow food. Moving to this new place was also about finding a different balance for myself in my own space. I did not want to get involved with Siddhartha Farm as this would have meant doing farming work full-time. I did not want to be consumed by farm work and have no energy for anything else. From the beginning I planned to work in the vegetable garden in the morning and have the rest of the day free for writing and painting. I wanted it to be a place where I could feel and work with the pulse of the earth but where I could also focus, dream, and create. I felt that I needed all those things for the new balance within my self and my life which I hoped to achieve. As I began to create my new space I started to understand that I was not just creating a vegetable garden but an environment where all aspects of my being could have expression.

Once I was clear about this, planning the practical details of the site and the buildings came easily and I went through the various processes to obtain the necessary permission to take care of the land. I started work on the land in April 2000 with the expectation of being ready to start growing when the first rains came in June/July. I decided to call the place 'Buddha Garden' which I thought was congruent with Siddhartha Farm and Forest of which it was a part.

******

The first job on the land was to clear it of all the eucalyptus trees, this being carried out by a work group of local men using very simple tools. As the trees came down and the pile of wood and leaves got larger it felt as if the land was starting to breathe again. I was also breathing more freely as with this first job on the land being started, I felt myself moving towards a new place and hopefully a different balance and way of being. At the same time I felt very shaky and vulnerable; rather like a wobbly jelly stepping on slippery stones that were themselves sliding around on the bed of a river. Would I be able to cope with the myriad things to be done and problems to be solved? I was helped by one of my dreams which showed me that if I tuned into my intuitive being, I would know the what-how-and-when of what to do so that everything would come together.

Just living one day at a time – when I could manage it – also helped.

Before the building work started I felt strongly to have a ritual on the land -- not only to ask for blessings on this new start but also to feel and harmonize with the spirit of the place. Just as the sun was setting, I lit incense and scattered flowers on each of the places where the buildings were going to be. It felt wonderfully quiet and peaceful. Suddenly, in the midst of this silence there was a tremendous noise and disturbance as a herd of cows with a black and white bull at their head came bursting through the fence very close to where I was standing. On seeing me the bull stopped short and stood there in all his potent power as we stared, eye-to-eye, for several minutes, the cows standing motionless behind him. The atmosphere seemed to fizz in the sudden silence.

We stood like that, staring hard at each other, for what seemed like a long time. Then something seemed to drain away and he just turned around like any ordinary animal and loped off with the cows following him. At the time I wondered if it had any special meaning, but as the place evolved it never became clear. In his confrontation and subsequent withdrawal, perhaps he was personifying the spirits of the place who were now willing that I should be there. Or perhaps he just didn't like me on his patch and when he found he couldn't make me go he did the only other possible thing.

The building work took place during the hottest months when the sun was beating down like a hammer and the air seemed to dance and burn around me. All my creative work was on hold, my days revolving around dealing with the numerous details essential to keep the construction work moving. First thing every morning I would walk across to the new land to look at and discuss the building work, about what was finished yesterday and what should be done today. Having started two new communities and built three houses in Auroville, I had a good idea of what I wanted and the simplest way to build it. At the same time I had to plan our solar-energy or power systems and decide how much energy my daughters and myself - really required. I needed to live with as simple a system as possible. What was more important? We decided that having a computer was essential whereas we were quite happy without a television, video, fridge or other electric kitchen equipment.

This was the seemingly small and confined focus of my life for many weeks. I had to keep reminding myself that the confinement I felt in one way was what was needed at this time to enable the greater freedom that I sought. As I walked back and forth between Siddhartha Forest and Siddharta Farm I took courage from the wide open expanse of the sky and the wide open possibilities that it seemed to be suggesting for me.

INNER SKY

My sky is the sky of the flatlands
A massive dome of soaring infinity.
Canvas for naked forces writ large and loud

My sky is my visible mantra.
A vast wilderness of possibilities
Witnessed in fluid eddies of illumination.

Let me have courage to rise, free and
Unbounded, into the immensity of my sky.
And fly, high and true.

For many days it would seem that very little was happening and then suddenly the shape of things to come would be evident. It was not only the shape of the buildings, both actual and projected, which I could see for the first time, but also the feeling of the place would be evident as well. Sometimes I had a kind of knowingness that this would be a good place to do all my different kinds of work. At other times I had such a lot of doubts and would question whether this was really a good move for me. At such times I felt as if I were at that point where the shore I was leaving had disappeared but that the shore I was going towards was only a hazy blob on the horizon. Often I had to remind myself, once again, to live day-by-day. To allow things to evolve rather than set deadlines and be too rigid about how I thought things should be progressing. Very often I found it hard to heed my own advice.

******

Although it was very hot and dry and the earth therefore very hard, I was, with the help of the large portable irrigation system from Siddhartha farm, able to start building the fence. Once completed, it provided a great feeling of protection, completely changing the vibration of the land as well as keeping all the animals off. With the fence in place I could begin to think carefully about how to set up the garden; how to lay out the beds and how to put in the necessary irrigation. With the garden becoming more solid I had a feeling of 'this is it' - 'it' being what I had wanted to do for so long.

With all the practical experience of several vegetable gardens, my work in the Farm Group, along with the inspiration of Paul, a Dutch farmer in Auroville at the time, I felt I knew enough about growing conditions and the practical jobs that would need to be done. I realised, however, that there would be a big difference between growing vegetables in a little garden for myself and growing vegetables in larger quantities for the community. While in my own garden I would go and pick whatever was available and use it as best I could. For the community I would have to think much more about what people wanted to buy. I intended to grow everything organically and would need to be aware of my growing schedule to make sure that I could provide an uninterrupted supply in sufficient quantities. And somehow I would have to do all this and be financially viable, especially if I employed someone to help.

These were just the practical details. I was sure there were other more subtle things I should probably have been thinking about, but at the time these practical concerns were all-consuming.

Then, at last, after what seemed like an unending hot season we had some rain. So very gentle it was and yet prolonged enough to soak the earth and produce that wonderful smell that comes when it rains after a long dry spell. With it I felt the promise of cooler weather and the cycles of the seasons continuing as if the earth were becoming animated and its heart beating. For me at that time the smell was the smell of life and the promise of continuation and a new life for myself.

All tied up as I was in my little concerns about the practicalities of the building and my own capacities to do the work, feeling, seeing, and smelling this life force came like a benediction that widened my perspective on everything. This was further enhanced when – with more rain – I was able to get 30 vegetable beds dug.

EARTH'S ASKING
Soft underbelly of
Moist upended soil
Just newly dug.

Earth

Inviting my hands
To sense its essence.
Empower its fruitfulness.

******

Months previously when I had first decided to move to Siddhartha Farm someone had asked me 'When do you think you will move?' and I had replied without thinking 'July 7th'. That turned out to be a very good date. It was one week after Emma returned from her holiday in the UK, and one week before she was due to go to her new school in Kodaikanal. For Rachael it meant that she would have finished moving before the start of the new school year in Auroville.

Rather than wait for all the buildings to be completed I began moving as soon as the kitchen and basic living space was habitable. I had been promised that everything would be finished by the 7th but when I looked at the bathroom on the morning of our moving day, my heart sank. There seemed to be so much still to do and I couldn't believe that it would be finished in time. All the arrangements had been made for moving, however, so there was nothing for it but to go ahead and hope that one way or another everything would work out.

As always the practical process of moving was exhausting. Several trips with the *vandi* (ox cart) were required, each time piled high with a wobbly heap of our belongings. I only moved the things needed for living - beds, bedding, and kitchen equipment. Everything connected with my work I left in Siddhartha Forest until the new work-room was ready in Buddha Garden. By the evening we had beds with sheets and pillows to sleep on and I had made our first meal. True to his promise the builder had finished the bathroom although he requested us not take a bath - otherwise the grouting keeping the tiles in place, would fall out.

Germination

I was so tired I slept like the proverbial log with, unfortunately, no dreams that I could remember. This was a pity as a dream on the first night spent in a new place is supposed to be particularly potent and full of meaning.

Living in the half-finished place in the middle of a building site and not having the work-room where I was living, became increasingly frustrating. The essential piece of paper always seemed to be in the other place.

Eventually I began to see the end of the physical move but there were maddening delays. The building of the second floor of the work room seemed to be going at snail's pace so that in the end I decided to make do with the roughest of finishing. The keet (thatch) roof over the building was then delayed by a huge thunder storm which required several sunny days to dry everything out before it could be re-started. The final moving day arrived and the last of my possessions were transported which, after three days of work, were eventually sorted out to my satisfaction. Following that, almost like a miracle, the solar power systems were moved and my work room was complete.

As if to welcome me, that evening, after a very grey day, the sun made an appearance to make a fabulous sunset which felt like a blessing and special light for my moving. This was also on the night of the full moon which I thought was very appropriate. As I soaked up the moonlight I thought how empty and tired I felt instead of the elation I thought I should feel.

MOON TOUCH
With no one to tell
But the moon

I whispered my heart-words
To her luminous, unblinking
Eye.

Her answer was
Moonshine.

Granted to all who
Would stand in
Her light.

How I Grew With My Garden

While I, in her
Luminosity.

Listened in vain, staring
At darkness, as pain
Twisted deep.

******

I started to work on the land with the words of an experienced Aurovilian farmer ringing in my ears:

'Every farmer has to work out the right balance for him or herself on a particular piece of land. On the same piece of land two people would find two different ways of creating that balance. You will find that some things will work and some things won't and what works for you won't necessarily work for someone else. It is a very individual process and you just have to keep working and reflecting and adjusting as necessary until eventually you find the right harmony for you.'

Looking at my diaries of this period I feel once again the raw energy of grappling day-by-day with many practical things which had to be tackled if the farm was to become viable. I was very aware that it was up to me to engage with the land and allow the land to tell me what it needed as much as for me to impose what I thought should be on the land given its characteristics. Each day as I worked with the garden I learnt a little more about how the balance between myself and the land might be achieved. This was not an easy task, especially in the beginning.

At the time I was moving onto the land, Arjunan, a Tamil Aurovilian, came to help me. With a family to support in Pondicherry, and having just passed through a difficult time, he came to work both from interest and the need to sort things out for himself. With his help I began planting some of the beds and little seedlings started to appear, but the ultimate results were very disappointing. We planted many seeds but the germination rate was not good, even for those seeds which had come in packets from the Government shop. Sometimes, only two thirds or even half of the plants came up and of those, many would fall prey to various poochies – that wonderful all embracing Tamil word for anything that crawled and flew and munched on our plants.

Even when the seedlings managed to overcome all the problems and grow into a producing plant they did not do very well. Some of the snake gourd plants were badly attacked by red *poochies* and as a result had very few functioning leaves. The cow pea beans, a tough plant that I had grown successfully elsewhere, also grew, but I had never seen them having to struggle like they were struggling in Buddha Garden. I found the garden such hard work for what seemed like very little return. It seemed that we were only able to grow very small amounts of vegetables, in contrast to most of the other Auroville farmers. Many were the moments when I felt very despondent and found that we were struggling as much as the plants were.

And yet, just when I thought I wouldn't be able to carry on I would get positive reinforcement from the most unexpected quarters.

One day at the end of a difficult morning I was standing looking at some spinach plants we had just put in which were all laying down on the soil looking rather limp in the hot sun. This beautiful butterfly came and settled on one of them. It felt like a benediction for both the plants and the earth with which we had been working that morning to help it become more alive.

Another time after a day of difficulties and rather dark thoughts there was a beautiful rainbow which came in the evening. They don't happen very often here but this one stayed in the sky for a long time, I think because of the setting sun which made the light go into the clouds at just the right angle. The colours were wonderful and the sky was luminously blue – almost ethereal.

These were the things that I tried to remember and carry in my heart as a sign that things weren't as bad as they sometimes appeared and that it was worthwhile to carry on.

******

So many times I was at my wits end to know what to do about the poochies. They attacked every part of the plant – leaf, flower, root and vegetable – and seemed to come from all sides – soil, air and water. Ladies fingers were particularly difficult as they were host to borers which came right inside the vegetable and were not always visible from the outside. It was so very disappointing. Once when Arjunan and I had cleared a pest-infested cucumber bed on which there were only a few plants and even fewer cucumbers, he said rather sadly, 'We're just growing food for cows'. I was glad that someone ate them and we did eventually get their milk, but I know what he meant.

A lot of advice came my way as to what I should use and we tried many different things to stop them, but nothing seemed to work very well. I put ash on the seedlings as I had done in Siddhartha Forest, but there was so much rain it kept getting washed off. Several times I rushed out with ash when the rain had stopped only to find that the poochies had beaten me to it. We tried using neem seeds, soaking them overnight and then using the water to spray onto the plants in the morning. Once again the rain made it difficult as it washed most of it away. Even when it didn't rain the poochies didn't seem to be too perturbed by it, jumping up as the spray hit them and then settling down again as the spray passed by. I hoped that the bitter taste of the neem spray made them eat less than they otherwise would although I didn't have too much evidence for this. Many plants had been chewed so much the leaves looked like lace.

******

The struggle to grow healthy plants along with the continuing battle with the poochies seemed to mirror the other battle I was having in order to make the place secure. The first time I had problems with stealing was during the first week after I had moved in. I went to paint one of the signs by the road and came back to find that someone had broken in and stolen some things from my capsule. A few weeks later I left the work room for only ten minutes to go over to the kitchen and when I came back I disturbed someone who was going through the cupboards. He ran away with my sewing things – this including a very nice pair of Wilkinson Sword scissors, unobtainable in India. The worst experience, however, was with the telephone cable.

The problems with this had started before we had even moved to Buddha Garden. It was arranged that the underground cable (we have no overhead telephone cables in Auroville) would be laid across the land between Siddhartha Forest and Buddha Garden. Permission was (we thought) duly sought and given from the land owner for this to happen. Once the cable was installed, however, his son, Velan, started to be very unpleasant towards us with violent demands for money. He maintained that his father should not have given permission because he had left the family to go and live with another woman elsewhere. It seemed that we had, unfortunately, been dropped into the midst of a family argument. Since payment was usually made to land owners when a cable was put across their land, this was quite a reasonable request, although in this case put in a very unreasonable way.

Eventually a sum was decided and agreed upon with Velan which I paid, but this did not stop the problems. He continued to harass me for money and cut the cable many times as a way of trying to force me to pay him more. Many times I would go to use the telephone, only to find it dead and would then have to go through the tedious process of getting it fixed. This meant cycling to find a phone from where I could tell the Telephone Service about the problem and then waiting for them to come and mend it. Each time the cable had to be dug up and the continual cutting and repairing greatly diminished the quality of the line. Living as I did in a fairly isolated situation I hated the cut off feeling which not having a telephone always seemed to give me. There was also the extra expense, of course.

The problems with Velan continued and he started to harass Herbert as well as myself, until I got the telephone cable re-laid so that it did not go across his land. As a result of this I decided to employ a watchman and although it helped, it was expensive and only partly effective.

Fortunately there was always the physical work in the garden that usually managed to restore some kind of balance within me.

****

One of the first things Arjunan and I did when Buddha Garden started was to create a nursery. In the beginning we put it under my capsule. I liked the thought of having our baby plants under the protection of my house, but we soon found it wasn't a good place as it was too shaded and as a result seemed to attract all manner of pests and diseases. Over the course of the first year the nursery was moved to many different places some of which turned out to be too hot, shaded at the wrong time of the day, or not having enough light. Eventually we found the right place where it has been for the last two years. It is in a very sunny place so in the hot season we protect the seedlings with a shade net. During the heavy monsoon rains the seedlings are protected with a polythene sheet - a special one that lets in the ultra violet rays of the sun so the plants can grow properly.

One thing we learnt was that it was best to grow all seeds in the nursery where they could be protected with nets from the pests. I remember being particularly pleased with the first bed of snake gourd we had planted using seedlings from the nursery. It was so satisfying to see a whole bed of plants without gaps and with plants that had not been eaten. The effort of growing them in the nursery and then replanting seemed to be worthwhile.
We now grow all our plants that way, even those that supposedly don't like being transplanted. When the seedlings are large enough we plant them out on the beds, covering them with nets if they are very delicate. Growing seeds

with protection like this seems to be the only way of stopping the pests from destroying them and making sure that the beds are full with growing and producing plants.

※※※※※※

Although I had hoped that Arjunan and I would do most of the work in the garden it soon became obvious that we needed help. This became acute when we started cutting the velvet beans, plants we had grown to bring nitrogen to the soil and which when cut make a very good mulch – a covering for the soil to protect it from hot sun and heavy rain. It was a dirty dusty job that was physically tiring and needed to be completed quickly. We had tomato and brinjal plants in the nursery ready for transplanting and if there was too much delay we would miss the best of the cool growing season.

I asked Herbert to find me some workers and two young men turned up one morning but they were a big disappointment. They needed constant attention to make sure they did the job as we wanted and they worked very slowly. I tried to engage their interest in various ways and got Arjunan to explain what we were doing and why as we all worked together. It didn't make any difference. They neither knew about nor appeared to have any interest in the work and they continued to work very slowly even when we did jobs together. They were slower even than Arjunan and I, and we didn't think that we worked particularly quickly.

I got very angry and eventually totally exasperated with them as it seemed the only way to get them to work was to hound them constantly and be very unpleasant. In the end we finished the velvet bean beds ourselves which took less energy than having to continually drive these workers along. It was such a relief when they went. I don't think my experience was particularly unusual as it is difficult to get good workers to do this kind of thing. I've known some very good farm and garden workers, but they seem to be few and far between and were usually already employed. Farm work is considered very low-status and only for those who haven't managed to do anything 'better'. Visiting other farmers I saw the enormous amounts of energy that was needed to make sure that the work was done properly.

I thought a lot about the sort of people I would like to help me. It seemed to me to be such a waste of time and energy to have people with no interest and who were just doing the job for the money. Arjunan and I discussed it a lot and then had the idea that maybe there were people out there who would like to volunteer to come and help us. At the time the guest season was just starting so we put up some posters and waited to see what would happen. We had several people come to help and it made such a difference, not only to the amount of work we were able to do but also to the feel of the garden. Working together with people who actually wanted to help seemed to create more energy than the sum of the individuals doing it. I found I had to watch them quite carefully though, and take care that they didn't do too much in the hot climate. Comparing myself to the volunteers I saw how much more used to the work I had become and how much I had adapted to the conditions. Enjoying their goodwill, interest and appreciation for what we were doing was, I found as important as their practical help.

******

Day-by-day over the first six months I could see the garden taking shape. Then we had a cyclone which literally turned everything topsy-turvey, both physically in the garden and within me. It started one night with wind and thin rain and by the next morning it was very overcast and grey. I got up much earlier than usual to pick what vegetables I could and was glad that I did as later it would have been impossible.

Throughout the day the wind gusted more and more fiercely. There was something very agitating about it and Emma said it made her feel as if she wanted to punch the wind. It was difficult to sit and do anything, not only because of the physical effects of the wind and paper blowing around everywhere, but because it felt so unsettling. During a lull Dirk came over to tell me that the windmill in Siddhartha Forest had broken. It had folded up - as it is meant to do under such conditions - but the wind had been so strong that it threw the folded up wheel against the tower and sheered it off. At least no one was hurt and this was one of several windmills in Auroville that had collapsed or broken.

The wind and rain continued all day and lying in my capsule that night I felt it shudder in the gusts although surprisingly I did not feel scared. The fact that it moved with the wind seemed confirmation that it would give with the wind and not break. Despite the howling wind, lashing rain, and my "excited"capsule, I went off to sleep and slept for most of the night. It was the calm that followed the cyclone passing over very early in the morning, which eventually woke me up.

There was damage everywhere -- trees had blown down and with them electricity and telephone cables. There was no electricity anywhere in the neighbouring village so women came to get water from us because the cyclone didn't affect our solar panels. Like everywhere else, both in Auroville and in the surrounding villages, the next day was spent clearing up. A lot of the drumstick trees that we had planted on the back beds had blown down but Arjunan managed to put most of them back up, tying them to other trees with rope to keep them upright. The wing beans, which had been growing up sticks and string, had blown down. Together we managed to get them upright again and I was surprised and very gratified to find there were still many growing despite the battering they had received. The plastic sheet we put up over the tomato seedlings in the nursery had shredded in the wind and as a result the little plants looked somewhat crushed, but we decided to plant them anyway in the hopes that at least some would survive. Some did.

All this destruction coming on top of all the other problems we had experienced made me wonder what I should do. Should I move? It seemed very soon to take such a drastic step, but if things were not going to work out I thought it was better to do it sooner rather than later.

How could I tell what was the right thing to do?

******

If growing vegetables was a problem, finding people who wanted to have them was also not easy. One morning, for instance, I started very early picking beans and found that for once we had a good amount. I felt so happy. Then after making several phone calls to various places it seemed that no one wanted them - they were the wrong kind of bean that no one liked. I got very angry and upset and started to cry and felt in the depths of despair. It had been so very difficult to grow those beans that no one seemed to want. Eventually, after a lot of phoning around, I did find someone - one of the guest houses - that took them. As I stood looking at the garden after Arjunan had taken the beans to be delivered, it occurred to me that the earth beds were mirroring my very self. They were exhausted and so was I. They needed nurturing and so did I. Clearly, I needed to care of myself as well as the earth.

Such an insight arising directly from my work in the garden was quite unusual. When I first came to Buddha Garden I had expected that the two different parts of my work - the garden and creative work - would somehow enhance each other, although I wasn't clear how this might happen. I felt that the work on the land and the development of the farm would be my anchor and the base from which my creative work would draw sustenance and inspiration. In reality, much of the time, the two parts seemed to be very separate, the practical demands of the garden seeming to have no relationship at all with my creative endeavours.

There were many days when I felt torn into little pieces by all the different jobs and organization that needed doing. More like I was flying through the air than working on the earth. So often I would start a job only to be called away to deal with something else. Where should the *vandi* driver put the compost he had just bought? When should he bring the straw for mulch? How much was I willing to pay? There were so many things needing my attention and concern which at that point could not be easily delegated to anyone else. So often these things would have nothing directly to do with growing vegetables but nevertheless needed my attention and action. I had to deal with the stealing and the problems with the telephone cable, not to mention the effort of finding a market for what we produced, as well as keeping track of and making sure that the cash continued to flow.

It was a paradox. It took so much of my energy to hold everything together and create the right environment for my creative work, that I had no energy left for the work itself. Where was the space I needed just to experience the garden and the sun and the wind and the sky? Often I hardly noticed it as I rushed around organising everything.

Except that somehow I continued to write and paint and, on occasions the different parts of what I did became intertwined. One morning I was standing in the garden and fell into quite a reverie about a collection of poems I was compiling – trying out different arrangements in my head, thinking about which pictures to use with which poems. Just dreaming away. It had taken me a long time to get started and until that point it had felt like swimming through mud. Now as I worked on the land, I suddenly saw how the poems and pictures could come together and felt much more enthused and able to complete it. I was astonished that I managed to do it with everything else that had been going on. It was as if something needed to be expressed and it did so, regardless. And that it was working in the garden that had made it possible.

Sometimes the work would be the anchor I needed in the midst of feelings of loneliness and depression and the consternation I felt about all the problems I was facing. One day, as I clipped the tomatoes, cutting off the side shoots so that all the growth would centre on the central stem, thoughts of my problems and the stresses and strains they induced were rolling around in my head. Gradually, however, without my being conscious of it, I became totally absorbed in what I was doing and completely silent with an inner stillness. It was an instant of utter peace and at-one-ness. Being absorbed in the moment all my problems ceased to exist. The memory of it stayed with me for the rest of the day with such gratitude for the garden that, whatever the problems, it gave me this.

******

Growing mainly local vegetables and not being able to grow large quantities of anything, finding a market for what we produced continued to be a challenge. What we could grow was not it seemed what people wanted to eat. One of the first of our regular customers was the café at the nearby Visitors Centre who used our vegetables for their daily 'organic dish of the day'. I liked the way the distinctive qualities of our vegetables were used for special meals and appreciated for that. Fortunately the quantities needed by the Visitors Centre were small as I continued to fret about our limited production. We rarely if ever were able to produce enough for the Solar Kitchen and sometimes the amounts we produced were so small it didn't seem worthwhile taking them all the way to Pour Tous (the Auroville distribution center) on the other side of Auroville.

I can't now remember where I got the idea for what I called 'the mixed bag scheme', but I expect it was when I read about the box scheme used by many organic farmers in the west. I had been thinking about it in a very unfocused way for some time when one day I just happened to mention it in passing - as something to think about - to Arjunan. Would there be anyone interested in having a bag of mixed vegetables – whatever we could grow – each week? He happened to mention it in passing to a friend who came the next day to ask if he could have one regularly every week. Later on I talked about the idea to a few other people and within a very short time I had several people signed up for a regular delivery. I just loved the way it happened – organically - without my having to push and hassle and expend energy which is what I felt I was having to do with everything else in the garden. I was already growing small quantities of a variety of things and this way of distributing them seemed much more appropriate to what I was actually doing.

As time passed and I got to know the people better who wanted the mixed bags I found that I liked this way of working. To pick vegetables for known individuals who wanted and appreciated our organic food felt so different from our previous way of doing things. I had a relationship with them and they with me. We appreciated each other and what we brought to the exchange. It also meant that I did not have to worry about whether I was growing enough of anything and really small amounts could be sold as part of a mixed bag rather than, as in the beginning, eating it ourselves. Maybe it was just as well that I hadn't been able to grow enough for the Solar Kitchen in that it had enabled me to do this which I found mutually very satisfying.

With these changes I felt a transformation in the garden, as if it were slowly evolving. This I thought was a better description than 'coming together' because I'm not sure that it ever did or has. I also felt happier growing smaller quantities of more of a variety of things rather than beating myself on the head because I couldn't grow enough for the Solar Kitchen or Pour Tous. Now my focus was on growing enough food for everyone who had asked for a mixed bag. Frequently I would worry that there wasn't enough, especially as the weather started to get hotter in April and May and the things we could grow became fewer. Yet somehow we managed to find something for everyone. Often I was in awe of how much we grew in this garden despite all the problems. Even as the temperature rose and there were fewer vegetables, we still had enough for everyone's mixed bags.

******

From the very beginning I wanted to make Buddha Garden financially viable, and from the outset focused on trying to make enough money to cover Arjunan's 'maintenance'. As an Aurovilian, he received this fixed monthly amount from the Central Fund which is supposed to cover basic needs and be independent of whatever work one is doing. Arjunan was of the opinion that so long as Central Fund paid his maintenance, we didn't have to worry about whether what we produced was enough to cover it or not, but I disagreed.

I felt that we should think about whether we were producing enough to cover his maintenance otherwise the energy flow would not be sustainable. I thought it was important to create something that was financially self-supporting. I didn't want a black hole into which money (probably mostly mine) had to be poured to keep it going. If I was not able to grow vegetables in a way that produced enough money to support it then I would have to look to see what this meant. Perhaps I needed to manage things more effectively or I needed to think of creative ways of finding financial support, perhaps be more open to magical ways of attracting money.

Wanting to be financially viable was not the only thing I was working for, but it was part of being self maintaining on all levels. If I wanted to have a really good vegetable garden I knew that I also needed to co-operate with nature. That it was not a question of doing this or doing that but relating to the totality of earth, plants and weather - observing the plants and then responding appropriately. I needed to do effective work – but what was that? How did it relate to the feelings I had about the earth and working with the natural rhythms? How could I do it in a way that was nourishing to me as well as the earth and kept the energy flowing on all levels? What was the role of money in all of this?

******

At the end of the year and with the guest season in full swing; more and more volunteers came to help. Many people just dropped in for a few mornings and seemed to appreciate the opportunity, if only for a short time, to be part of the practical work of building Auroville. Others came for longer periods and I had two university students who were part of a group from an American university doing a course here. They learnt how to do the jobs very quickly and as a result became extremely useful, eventually helping other less experienced volunteers with the work.

With so many more volunteers I found that I was working in a different way. It required a clear focus to organise everything so that the work got done and everyone was doing something according to his or her capacity and hopefully enjoying themselves. Over the months I found the volunteers bringing such uplifting goodwill that when we were all doing things together, a wonderfully caring and dynamic energy carried me along, especially at moments when I had been dealing with negative things like the severed telephone cable or someone making yet another hole in the fence.

The volunteers learnt from me but I also learnt from them. Khema, an ex-Buddhist nun, came to the garden very regularly and I learnt a lot from the quiet attentiveness and awareness that she brought to the work. As a result of being with her I became more conscious of the spiritual aspects of my work in this garden and saw that for me it was a kind of meditation. This being so I became more aware of how the energy and attentiveness that I brought to the work was an important dimension of managing it well. Paulo coming from Brazil and sharing his gardening experiences in a similar community at home helped give me a wider perspective and new ideas about the relationship between Buddha Garden and the community of Auroville. One morning an Aurovilian friend of Arjunan's came to help after which he went off to his work with a huge grin on his face saying that he had really enjoyed himself. I wished there were more people from Auroville who would make a connection with the land like this, but most were very busy with other things.

Many people seemed to be moved by working in Buddha Garden and for many the experience was very meaningful and sometimes transformative. I was always surprised to hear about this as it seemed to be a grace over which I, nor anyone else, had any control. I was also surprised by the number of people who felt, perhaps for the very first time, a strong relationship to the land. I didn't consciously feel such a strong relationship, maybe because I was too focused on 'what needs doing' all the time. Or perhaps living so close to the land it had permeated my being to the extent that it was so much a part of myself, like my hands or my heart, that I didn't feel the close relationship I had to it.

For many volunteers the heat was a problem. Some found it impossible to work outside towards the end of the morning and they had to be found jobs in the shade. Even those who had been in India for some time and thought of themselves as being used to the climate had problems. Often they had not done hard physical work in the heat and were surprised at the effects this could have on them. Arjunan and I thought it would be so much better for everyone if we could start working earlier when it was cool – which is the traditional way in this climate. To do this, however, we would have to supply breakfast as for most volunteers it was impossible to get an early breakfast especially when they were staying in a guest house. I worried about all the extra organisation this would entail – getting the food in, prepared, and then cooked. Something I couldn't do myself given all the other work I had to organise.

Eventually we found someone from the local village who was willing to come early and cook an Indian breakfast and this became another much appreciated focus within Buddha Garden. It was good to work and then enjoy some of the fruits of that work when we all sat round and ate together. I found the early mornings very special. I loved being in the garden at this time which I felt was the daily miracle of a new start and all the possibilities that might come with that.

INTO A HIGHER SKY

Namaste.
To dawn sun; bleeding
Into earth's sky rising
With the dawn of a higher
Sky; which lifts me to it's
Vastness.

It was good when the volunteers came but when most of them left for the hot summer months it enabled Arjunan and I to take things more easily and do things which weren't possible when we had so many people to organise. One day, when we were on our own, we just walked around the garden to observe what was happening. I enjoyed it and wished we could do it more often. Usually we were so focused on doing the next job – whatever that might be – that we rarely took the time to stand and stare and envision how we would like to see things change. We talked about what we would do during the next hot weeks and months, the season when there would be fewer people in Auroville and the plants would not grow so well. We decided it would be best to improve the soil by planting beans and making a lot of compost.

The next day we started doing that. We made a compost heap which I still love to do. I love the physicality of the work - the bending and stretching to pick up and put into a neat pile - I feel strong and rooted. I love the smell of the cow dung mixture as we slosh it onto the heap. I love knowing that we are helping the soil (I miss-spelt that the first time and put 'soul', which is not so far wrong I think). What I particularly liked this time was that, after a year, most of the material came from the garden. We were giving back something for what had been taken out. All part of creating that balance which was needed if the garden was to function well.

******

Several times during that first year I was asked to either talk or write about my experience. Buddha Garden also acted as host to pupils from the nearby Udavi School in the next village as well as students from Kodaikanal where my daughter was studying. As I showed them around and we talked a bit about organic farming and sustainability I felt how close to my heart this was and how much I wanted to share what I was doing with the next generation. Talking or writing I was often surprised at the passion I displayed, even when I was going through difficult practical experiences and feeling that my passion was spent.

I was aware how easily I got discouraged and how a simple thing like having a few extra people to help could make all the difference as to whether I felt I was coping or not. I did my best and I knew the standard of a lot of things was very low, but I felt it was the best I could do under the circumstances without running myself ragged. Which seemed to happen anyway. As the first year drew to a close I felt the garden growing, but at the same time I also felt as if I were running out of steam. I had set this place up, got it going and slowly things were improving. But it still felt as if I were pushing the mountain and I didn't know how much longer I could do it.

Looking at what we produced, it still did not seem very much. I saw that I needed to continue to tune in both to what was needed to produce good vegetables as well as what was wanted by the community – although I thought I might try and affect the latter by a bit by education about some of the eating possibilities of what we were growing. Provided I could find the energy from somewhere. Adjusting in this way, was, I felt a lesson in what I needed to do in the rest of my life – sense the energies and go with them instead of railing against them and getting all resentful.

The cactus does not curse the sun
But grows a thick skin, thick
With spikes to shield her
Inner core.

The cactus does not mourn the drought
But gladly greets the dew,
Absorbing its precious drops
Of moist coolness.

Thus she takes the moment
To create dawn flowers of
White pristine freshness
In a husk dry world.

And when they shrivel as the sun climbs
She does not blame the heat or bewail
Their transient beauty, but releases them,
Freely, to the baking earth.

And turning inward, she rests in the
Dark secret roots of her fecundity.

I felt that the balance I had tried to achieve in my life, with time for writing and painting and dreaming, was very elusive. There were all the difficulties of security and the telephone cable problems which took up so much of my time and energy. There were so many things to attend to that often the inner voice seemed to have been completely overpowered with all the outside noise and interference. Was it really possible to grow the food necessary for our survival, but also have time and space to dream and create in other ways?

Something I also realised in the course of the first year was that it was not just a question of growing vegetables but of growing them with a particular awareness and consciousness. More and more I realised that growing the food we needed to live was not just about producing calories. I saw that our vegetables had a special energy that nourished us on many levels. That doing this work was not just about completing garden tasks. It was also about bringing a certain level of awareness and love to infuse the work while consciously working with the energies of the earth and creation. For this reason working with volunteers – usually people who had an interest and came with a special energy -- became more and more important. It was this special energy which was celebrated at the breakfast where we all sat down to eat together after work.

Yet at times the journey felt too difficult and unsatisfying; perhaps I was too focused on results rather than the journey itself. Perhaps it was the opportunity to do this work which was its own reward and anything else – like making a success of it - was just a bonus. If I were to enjoy what I was doing and produce some vegetables, wasn't that enough? Wasn't it the journey that was important and not the destination?

I was thinking about all these things one day when I opened our community newsletter and saw the following quotation from the Mother:

'the perfectly pure aspiration that doesn't expect any result – absolutely free from the slightest idea of result – the aspiration in its essential purity……that's not frequent'

This was part of a whole piece about giving, and how according to her, it is this which is important, not whether we get what we want. Funny how I never knew the Mother personally or felt a very strong connection with her, but often I get these really pertinent comments from Her at just the right time.

****

Germination

On the first day of May I had a horrible shock which reverberated through me for a long time. A thief had broken into my capsule and gone through all my things, turning the bed over, opening my trunk and throwing everything around. Given the insecure situation I kept nothing of value in the capsule except the tape recorder which was locked to one of the big struts with a chain and padlock. The thief had found the key so the tape recorder was gone. I got a grim satisfaction from imagining the thief's consternation when he eventually found that the tape recorder wouldn't work. It was very old, second or third-hand, and I was thinking of getting a new one as it was not repairable.

I felt totally violated and couldn't sleep. I felt I had had enough of living in conditions where nothing was safe and where I felt so continuously under siege, even after taking what practical measures I could to become more secure. I hated living with the feeling that one lapse in security on my part would lead to someone getting in and taking my things as had happened this time with my capsule.

I spent a lot of time thinking about what else I could do to feel more protected, from making the entry into my capsule more difficult by putting bars up at the windows to enclosing the open space where I did my painting. I didn't keep anything of value there but I felt it was only a matter of time before someone vandalised my paintings as they had vandalised my capsule. I could do all this, but I didn't want to feel that I had to seal myself behind bars to be secure. As these ideas went round and round in my head seemingly with no solution, I saw that one reason for this kind of thinking was that it was a sort of defence against the terrible feelings of vulnerability which made me feel utterly desperate and depressed.

The despondency brought on all the other negative feelings I had about what I was doing and the huge difficulties there seemed to be in every part of my life – from the poochies that ate all my vegetables to my seeming inability to create a supportive environment in which to do this work.

I thought long and hard about why I was in this situation. Was there a lesson I needed to learn? Within the situation I saw various echoes from my childhood, in particular my need to do something 'useful' in order to be loved, but it was not just that. It was not just that I was re-creating an aspect, or even a whole configuration of things I had experienced in my childhood. It seemed to mirror something much deeper within me.

I had moved to this new place and had worked so hard to change the things that I felt needed changing in my life. That I should live alone or at least with the potential to live with someone more supportive than Dirk. That I should arrange my life to focus on what I felt was really important and to create an environment where I could do this more easily. That I would give as much importance to my creative and inner life as I did to my outer 'useful' life and that I would make a situation where all of these parts of me would find adequate expression.

I had made these changes and created what I thought was a new situation. Yet I was still facing a situation with very strong echoes from my childhood suggesting that there was something within me which was still refusing to change despite my going through the motions of doing so.

It came to me one night that although I had made these outer changes – and even though they were the result of inner movements – somehow at the core I did not believe in myself. It wasn't a question about whether I believed in myself enough to 'do' my gardening, creative work or whatever successfully; nor was it a question about whether I was organising my life in a way that enabled me to focus on what I thought was important. It was more about my deep feeling of being worthwhile just being myself. In one way I was going against the very strong conditioning I had experienced as a child that unless I did something useful (in a practical sense) then I was not worthwhile or lovable. 'Useful' work was practical and often meant that I acted in a masculine rather than a feminine way of being. Doing practical things in a masculine, outer practical way, was better and more important than being in a feminine, inner feeling way.

I saw that I was still denigrating my female inner feeling way of being and in a deep sense did not accept (I had great difficulty finding the right word here – 'believe', 'trust', 'convinced of my worth') myself as a woman. As a being, in a female way of being. My inner female was still under siege from my masculine self and this was mirrored in the outer world.

******

This inner turmoil was mirrored in the outer turmoil of an unusually violent storm. I woke up to rain and wind lashing into and whirling around inside my capsule making me very wet. I lay awake for a long time listening to the loud thunder and watching the lightening rent the sky. It was so very violent and seemed to mirror the violence I felt had been done to me by the thief and the subsequent outrage I had felt towards him.

Germination

Lightening struck the kitchen and Rachael's room. It also struck and completely annihilated my telephone cable - the new one that I thought was safe from Velan had been destroyed by nature.

It seemed that violence was in the air. The day after the storm Arjunan came to work very late. It was partly the storm but partly a bad fight that occurred in the village near to the Auroville community where he lived. Two gangs had been on the rampage, one person was killed, and more destruction promised.

******

During the heat of the hottest month of the year, I thought long and hard about whether I would stay in Buddha Garden or not. The garden seemed to be more or less working but nothing else did and I was starting to have panic attacks - a result I think of the strain under which I was living. The work calmed me but otherwise I felt very on edge and vulnerable.

Was it a question of fighting harder or should I give up altogether?

It was while these things were – once again going around in my head that Murthi from the neighbouring village came to see me. Over the months he'd carried out some carpentry work for me and was visiting to see if I had anything else for him to do.

He'd always shown a lot of interest in what I did in Buddha Garden because as a boy he used to come and work on that particular piece of land. We got talking about it again and he described how he had often ploughed this land while a boy. His father owned the plough and bullocks and during the period of the first rains, after three good rainfalls, he would be waiting for the call to come and plough. It would come one morning very early – 3.00am - and he would have to get up, hitch the plough to the bullocks and start work. He would have to work very hard to get the work completed as soon as possible before the land dried out, starting work while it was dark and carrying on until around 11.00am. After a break he would start once more at 3.00pm working until about 5.00pm depending on how much there was to do. He was paid three rupees per day for ploughing but this was for feeding the bullocks. The main payment was a part of the harvest. Much less money was used then than now and the harvest was the really valuable payment for this work.

On the fields where I was growing vegetables and had built my house, he remembered them growing a variety of crops including rice, ragi, and sorghum. There was no irrigation so a good crop depended on the rains, although many of the maize crops would grow with very little water. I was very interested to know what they did about *poochies?* Did they find them as much of a trial as I did? He said they used a 'white powder' for everything, which I have a horrible suspicion was probably DDT as it is still used by some village farmers here indiscriminately.

A few years ago the family that owned the land stopped growing crops on these fields. Murthi said this was because of a shortage of rain, but there were also other factors which made it less worthwhile. Cows eating the crops became much more of a problem. Traditionally cows were cared for by young children who kept them under control, but, as more children went to school, cows were turned out to fend for themselves. Paying someone to look after the cows was beyond most people's means and paying for a watchman to stop the cows eating the crops was also too expensive. As Auroville grew, more villagers worked there or in Pondicherry, earning money to buy food rather than growing it themselves. Given all the problems of growing food and with government encouragement, more land was used for growing cash crops - trees like casuarina, eucalyptus, and cashews. They needed little maintenance, were not eaten by cows, and provided a good income after a few years. This wasn't always the case as a few years previously casuarina wood was so cheap it cost more to cut it down than for what it could be sold. The price of cashews too fluctuates according to the world market, and at times could be very low.

The family who originally owned this land, like many other people, stopped growing food and planted it with eucaplyptus. This was about fifteen years ago. Some years later, maybe to pay for a wedding or a house, they sold the land to Auroville.

Hearing all this I felt for this piece of earth in a way that I had never done before. Using chemicals and then growing eucalyptus must have taken away most of the soil's nutrients. No wonder the soil was so poor and I had found it so difficult to grow food.

I saw the land as a living entity with a history much longer than that which Murthi described. I saw it stretching back into the distant past. To the land as it was when it was farmed by the family and before that, the forest that it used to be. In the aeons of time that this land had existed, my time with it was less than the blink of an eyelid. Not enough time to repair the damage of the last hundreds of years when the forest was destroyed and a desert took its place. Not enough time to repair the soil so that it became productive enough to grow food.

I saw that empowering the earth was not something that could be achieved in a short time or to a timetable of my making. The work I had done with this land during this first year was only a beginning -- an infinitesimal first step towards healing its wounds and restoring it to life.

I felt the earth calling me to continue what had barely begun. I felt a deep rightness about what I was doing, despite all the obstacles and often the feeling that everything was too difficult for me to stay. I felt in my heart that my journey continued by staying in Buddha Garden– at least for a little while longer.

INNER SEA

My sea is the fathomless ocean
Of churning currents felt
In bottomless depths

My sea is the ocean untamed
Of wild engulfing waves in
Savage, screaming storms.

Dare I plumb the depths of this
Infinity?
Go naked into its moving
Vastness?
Submerge myself,
Opened?

PART THREE

BECOMING

CREATION AND DESTRUCTION

Thinking about Buddha Garden and whether I should stay or go it felt as if there were two rivers within me. One flowed out of Buddha Garden towards a less difficult and demanding life, from which emerged a lot of agonizing about my loneliness, lack of support, and whether this was what I could or should be doing. The other flowed deeper, both into the land and within myself towards the continuation of the work already begun and the transformation that it stirred within me. It was from this deeper mystery that Buddha Garden seemed to be shaped.

Having acknowledged to myself, although with some reservations, that I would continue in Buddha Garden, I began the second year concentrating on things that would facilitate the practical work. The most important of these was to build a store room. By this time the amount of equipment and tools were starting to take over the kitchen which was the only secure place we had to put them. Everything was packed closely together on two shelves and it was very difficult to keep everything organized and in place. All too often, sometimes several times in a morning, we would find ourselves unpacking everything to get at one very necessary tool which had been put right at the back, under everything else.

We started to build a store room and cycle shed with a covered verandah to weigh and pack the vegetables, in addition to a room on the first floor for Emma. Up to that time we had weighed our produce in one corner of the kitchen and as the diversity and amounts of what we produced increased it was clear that we needed a larger space. At the same time we also, in collaboration with Siddhartha Farm where cows were kept, built a cow urine system. We were greatly encouraged in this by Paul who thought that it would help increase production as well as make better use of the cow urine which up to then had just run out of the cow shed onto a patch of cow grass. Cow urine has high nitrogen content and is therefore very good for plants, especially leafy things like spinach. We built a large holding tank close to the cow shed to collect the urine as it ran out from the central gutter. A series of pipes connected the holding tank to the tank in Buddha Garden and a pump was purchased to pump it through. We then used very long hoses to put it onto the vegetable beds.

To improve security, the fence at the bottom of the garden was replaced by granite pillars and wire. This was stronger than the original fence made of bamboo panels which had been knocked over a number of times by overloaded lorries carrying wood from nearby plantations. At the same time

I decided to move the gate from the bottom of the garden to a place just beyond the store room where I could see it more easily. With this and the continuing use of a watchman I did feel somewhat more secure although this feeling was very fragile. On one occasion a friend I had staying with me forgot to lock her door when she went out. Seeing my subsequent feelings of anxiety showed me how insecure I was feeling. Once the store room was finished I, with some regret, decided that I would change my art room as well to make it more secure. It was a beautiful open space – just right for painting – but with the security situation being what it was I felt that it was only a matter of time before I had something stolen or vandalized.

In the end I was very pleased with the finished buildings; the art room seemed to retain its feelings of spaciousness despite the windows and door and I loved working in the large covered area downstairs in front of the store room, sorting and weighing the vegetables. And of course it was very good to have a safe and ordered space for all the tools, other garden equipment and bicycles

******

At this time of consolidation I started to write about my experiences of the first year. Reading my diaries of that time I was surprised to see how inspiration for that book came at a time of extra work and stress, at the start of a new cycle, in exactly the same way as has happened with writing this book. Why is it that inspiration comes at such inconvenient times?

Around that time I had many dreams which seemed to confirm that I should somehow find time for writing. One image was of myself as a very thin worm eating through compost and in the process growing larger. When the worm had digested and created a large amount of very fine soil a pair of hands scooped it up and placed it where the soil was exceptionally poor. Here it dispersed, in the process making the poor soil more potent.

I understood the image to be showing me that I must digest the material I had been writing until it became, like the image of the fine soil, a more refined thing with the capacity to inspire (make more potent) others. The work of growing during this process mirrored the growth in understanding that I often feel as I write. That in the act of putting words on paper I am helped to see more clearly what is going on within and without and what is needed holistically both for myself and my situation. Writing about the first year reaffirmed for me that, despite the difficulties, I wanted to continue with Buddha Garden - at least for another year.

It also helped me to see what I was doing in the wider context of the longer history of this land and the future. Any increase in the fertility of the soil would help future generations on this patch of earth even if I didn't manage to make the garden financially viable or grow sufficient vegetables in the time I spent here. I had to keep reminding myself that what I was trying to do was a very long term process; it took a hundred years or more to strip the soil of its fertility and will probably take much longer than that to completely restore it.

******

I felt that the work in the garden had achieved a certain rhythm and that we had learnt to do a lot of things more successfully. During the hot season we had had to suspend the mixed bags as we were producing so little but once the first rains had arrived we started clearing, composting, mulching and planting beds. We used a variety of vegetable seedlings that we had now successfully grown under nets in the nursery during the hot weather. At last the garden started to look green with many beds full of healthy plants. With the arrival of our first pumpkins we were able to start the mixed bags again after a two-month gap. The first morning we did it I felt wonderful and it reminded me of why I do this work. One morning, looking at the beds of growing plants, I felt, maybe for the first time, that the energy of Buddha Garden had got to a point where the energy was carrying me rather than me carrying it. I was aware though, of the obviously still huge amounts of work to do.

My confidence about the vegetable growing was, however, juxtaposed with brutal assaults on my feelings of security. One day I returned from a trip to Pondicherry to find that a thief had visited my capsule yet again. This was despite my watchman being there the whole time I was away. This time the thief had wrenched off the handle of the box (which was chained with lock to one of the major struts) where I kept my walkman and tapes and gone off with it. What was most worrying was that the nature of these thefts indicated that the thief knew when I was going out and so was presumably keeping watch on my movements as well as those of the watchman who couldn't be everywhere at all times. It was also peculiar that the dogs never seemed to be upset by this intruder so it was probably someone known to them.

My feelings of vulnerability and insecurity became almost unbearable. I felt as if I were a target of violation. I tried hard to keep everything in perspective and not feel totally overwhelmed so as not to get onto the slippery slope down towards depression again. Physically, for several days I felt numb and stiff and was hardly able to move my back and hips. Our black dog was a perfect mirror of that part of me. At the time she was being terrorised by the male dog and at one point I saw her sitting like a lump of jelly frozen with fear and unwilling to move. When she stood up she gave a new meaning to the expression 'hang dog' - everything about her drooped and I felt exactly how she looked.

*****

The line between my coping and not coping seemed to stretch thinner and thinner. Several mornings running the kitchen helper did not turn up and I had no choice but to cook breakfast for the volunteers who came to work that morning. This was not a job I could easily delegate to someone who did not know the kitchen or the sort of food we cooked. I enjoy cooking, but trying to do that while also trying to organise the work and do all the other things which were needed felt – and probably was – more or less impossible. I was running between the garden and the kitchen and felt that I was not doing anything very adequately.

I loved the energy, optimism and goodwill that volunteers brought, but some organisation was necessary on my part if this were to be optimised and the work enjoyed by everyone. As the anchor in Buddha Garden it was me that had to facilitate this. Most of the volunteers came with little or no experience in doing this kind of work and those that did have experience were not used to this environment. The things we grew and the tools we used were all unfamiliar and for some the climate was very trying, even working as we did early in the morning to take advantage of the coolness. Organising the volunteers – seeing who was capable of doing what needed to be done and making sure that everyone had a job that they could do and enjoy doing – had become a much more important task.

In addition to volunteers, increasing numbers of visitors were coming at all times of the day to have a look at what we were doing, some of them wanting to talk. More and more of my time was spent doing this and it was becoming an increasing burden especially when visitors arrived in the afternoons when I was writing or painting. I wanted Buddha Garden to remain open but it was clear that unless something was done I wouldn't have time to do the garden work let alone write and paint. To deal with this I created an information board so that visitors could find the information they needed without having to talk to me. This made a big difference and if people really wanted to see me they could make an appointment. It was also a relief not having to keep repeating myself; sometimes when telling people for the umpteenth time about how Buddha Garden was set up I was very unnerved to observe that while certain words were coming out of my mouth, my mind was miles away working on my writing or the latest practical problems that had to be resolved.

As more people came I felt a sense of relentlessness, and paradoxically, it seemed to increase the sense of real loneliness that I felt. So many of the people coming to see me were coming to Buddha Garden on the way to somewhere else and often wanted something from me, usually information about what I was doing and why. I longed for there to be someone else with whom to share all the responsibilities.

******

Every since my partner had died I had missed having another adult with whom to share my life. Little things would bring on acute feelings of loneliness and desolation. So often I felt that something necessary to my life was missing and that I couldn't go on without it. Yet I did because I had to - for my daughters. I sometimes wondered if some of my feelings of loneliness, despair and emptiness were unplugged from the land. More and more as I worked on the land I saw how much it had been plundered of its life energy and how it was too exhausted to produce very much.

I still wished to do this work with others and my inability to either find or create a community of like minded people made me at times very despairing. After the failure of all my community experiments I had hoped that by following my own energy which led to Buddha Garden and building up an energy field there, others with a similar focus would be attracted. To some degree this had happened except that I found the engagement I was able to have with them was usually fleeting (sometimes very fleeting) and the extent to which I could share with them was limited. Many people came to Buddha Garden but few wanted to stay for any length of time and no one wanted to share the total commitment with me. Neither going out and looking for the right people and creating a community or creating a place where the right people might come seemed to work.

It was difficult to know how to respond in this situation since there didn't seem to be any further practical things I could do. Wallowing around in my pain and despair and knowing that there were few people with whom I felt deeply in tune made me unappreciative of what I did receive. There was Arjunan who had decided to stay after the first year and had become more and more involved with the work as well as a few others who gave me warmth and love at particular points when it was needed.

For a gentle touch
Freely given

For a true word
Precisely imparted
For an unflinching heart
Generously listening

For knowing these benedictions
In the desolate wastes of my
Grieving soul.

Deo gratias.

Weeding in the garden one morning I was thinking about being alone and living on my own and wondering why I was in the situation at this time. I could see what freedom this aloneness could give me, to develop at my own pace and in my own way without having to worry about someone else. I saw how often in the past I had been with people and in situations where I had changed and they had not. How often they had not been able to accept the changes within me so I had to leave if I were not to be stifled by them. Despite the often painful process of leaving, it was usually a time of learning and growth for myself.

Had I reached the limits of growth through such ways? Perhaps being alone would present me with an alternative and maybe greater possibility for growth …….. or maybe it was just different and what I needed for now…. But the loneliness still hurt.

******

And then came Kent, who turned up unexpectedly one morning and cheerfully asked me what needed doing. When I told him that it was a weeding day he happily rolled up his sleeves and joined in with everyone else. When we re- mulched the bed with straw he proffered some suggestions for my consideration about how this could be done a little differently to optimize the quality of the soil on the bed. He displayed a keen interest in everything that was going on and asked some very pertinent questions which got me thinking about what I was doing and whether I was doing everything in the best possible way given the situation. Gradually as I got to know him I found out about his own farm in South Africa and the considerable expertise and experience he had in general farming, permaculture, and community building in a place where the climate was very similar to that of Auroville.

As we started to discuss the farm he began to draw out ideas that I had had going around in my head in a sort of formless way. He seemed to be able to tune in to something within the deeper river of myself that was there but of which I was only semi conscious. He was then able to help me bring it to consciousness and eventually manifestation. More land had become available around Buddha Garden and although I had made no decision about whether to take it up or not I did have a few ideas about how it might be incorporated with what I was already doing.

One of the things that I felt concerned about was that with the line between coping and not coping being so thin whether it was a good idea to contemplate taking on more land. Kent was very bracing about this and said that it all depended on me. He said that I should see the farm as an energy system and that all the time I needed to be aware about how I used my energy in conjunction with all the other energies so that more energy becomes available – to be expressed in how much we produced. He said that the energy was limitless but for that to manifest we had to have a right connection with the land. To get that it was not enough to 'work hard' (although that might be needed) but to be constantly aware of what was going on and to use all our resources, especially ourselves, intelligently.

To see how this might be created in Buddha Garden we walked together one afternoon over the land. Kent said that I needed to see how to relate all the activities of the farm so that they supported each other. He felt that the farm should have a variety of activities not all of which needed as much intensive work as the vegetable garden. It was also important that things that needed a lot of attention were close to where I lived, so that I couldn't help but see them every time I came out of the house, whereas things needing less attention could be further away. We talked at length about my ideas for an integrated chicken project where there would be a series of rotation yards which would be used for growing vegetables when the chickens were not using them. The idea was that the chickens would be able to get more food while at the same time improving the soil with their manure. I had always been very concerned about the cost of setting up such a project as with the animals and people who might attack the chickens it would have to be a fairly substantial building which could not be done cheaply. Kent, who suffered from similar problems in his own farm, said that he had built such a project and that it was worthwhile and eventually financially viable. To hear him say that gave me a lot of confidence to go ahead and the chicken project has turned out be very good for Buddha Garden, providing us with a good source of manure, free range eggs, chicken meat and an improved soil in which to grow vegetables. The first one was so successful that we recently decided to build another.

As these new ideas crystalised I asked Kent if it were really going to be possible for me to run this place on my own as it seemed as if there would be a lot of extra work. He said I must be very clear about how much work I wanted to do. I could if I wished create a place where I grafted for ten to twelve hours a day or a place where I only needed to work in the mornings. It was up to me to know what I wanted and to plan accordingly. We were standing in the vegetable garden as we talked about this. 'Is there anywhere we can sit?' asked Kent looking around. Of course there wasn't as the idea of there being enough time to just sit had never crossed my mind. Kent also reminded me that as well as places to sit it was also good to have a healing garden as well as sacred spaces. The farm was not just a place of work but also a place of contemplation and connection with other energies. Subsequently, I made provision for all of this although I probably don't use them as much as I should.

Together we drew up a plan for the further development of Buddha Garden as a fully fledged farm. Next to the vegetable garden was a piece of land that was to become an orchard. The chicken project would be put beside this as being further from the outer fence would hopefully deter would be thieves. In the land behind the houses a cashew plantation was planned which would eventually bring in a cash crop for the things that we were not able to produce ourselves. Behind that was to be the stone circle which was our sacred space. Beyond that in the two areas most remote from the houses we would plant a wood lot, growing trees that didn't mind standing in water as it flooded during the monsoon. The other flat area, which also flooded, would be used for growing cereals. At that point I was hoping that we could use this land for growing all the food for our chickens, but so far we haven't achieved this. All along the side of the farm a small forest would be planted which would provide us with material for compost as well as making a buffer between the path going on the outside of the fence and the main areas of the farm.

It sounded, and turned out to be, a lot of work with the rest of the year being taken up with the implementation of these plans.

******

In February of this, our second year, we sold more vegetables and had the highest turnover we had ever experienced. I started the new building for the chicken house as well as the fencing and other work that would eventually turn Buddha Garden into a fully fledged farm. In February on Mother's birthday (a special day in Auroville) I stood in morning mist looking at the trenches which had been dug ready to start building the chicken house. I felt everything coalescing into a real farm almost despite myself. I also felt that everything was moving towards something that was more than just about me as an individual. That there was a wider purpose to what I was trying to do here.

I felt this again a few days later when, one morning as we started work, Arjunan and I found to our surprise that we were on our own. Uncharacteristically there were no volunteers and the kitchen helper had taken the day off to go to a wedding. We had a wonderfully quiet morning in the garden together. It was such a change to do the work at our own pace, to talk more freely without having to worry about keeping volunteers busy and happy. We were in the giddy situation of not having to do any work at all if we didn't feel like it.

We therefore decided that as a treat we would go out for breakfast in the 'hotel' in the village. This turned out to be the usual dark room with rickety tables and chairs and a sooty ceiling marked with white dots to keep off the evil eye. In the darkest corner, the plates of idlies and pots of sambar and pickle were set out underneath a high dusty altar hosting pictures of Hindu gods and goddesses. Seeing us come in the owner hastily cleaned up one of the tables which looked as if it had recently been used for cooking. We were given prime position under the one and only fan – working it appeared from thin wires that looped under the eaves and across the ceiling of the room.

When the food came I was surprised to see it served on the top of plastic covered stainless steel plates. Very peculiar. What was wrong with just washing the plates and then reusing them? According to Arjunan this would not be acceptable, and not only because the place had no running water, so plate washing would not be very thorough. There was the question of ritual cleanliness. If plates were going to be used by people of different castes, this was only acceptable if the food was served on a plate covered with something which could be thrown away afterwards. The traditional way of doing this was to use banana leaves, but as Arjunan explained, this is now too expensive for such places; plastic is much cheaper, can be bought by the kilo and there are no worries about whether it is fresh or not. It was obviously the thinnest and cheapest plastic so I didn't like to dwell on what may have been leaching into the food from it – best to eat as quickly as possible so the food didn't spend too long sitting on it. There didn't seem to be a way around this problem for the hotel owner who was obviously running the place on the thinnest of shoe strings. Maybe the two plates that he gave to Arjunan and myself were the only two plates he possessed.

After we finished we looked out at the back yard and saw the sad results of using all that plastic. With banana leaves all one has to do is throw them out in a heap where the cows and goats will eat what they can and the rest will turn into compost. Here they had treated the plastic as if it were banana leaves and although it looked as if the cows and goats had eaten what they could, the remaining plastic was left there to blow around and make a horrible mess with shredded bits blown into the nearby trees and bushes.

It was as I looked at this that something ignited within me. I thought 'We can't go on treating the earth like this'.

It wasn't that I felt I could necessarily do anything in this case. Clearly there were delicate social and other factors, not within my power to change at the given moment, that would have to be negotiated and addressed. But looking at the mess I didn't feel quite so hopeless and empty about the work I was doing in Buddha Garden. Was it because I saw this work as part of a wider movement? Was my compassion for the earth re-ignited? I really don't know except that when I came back to the garden I did not feel quite so empty.

Funnily enough it reminded me of the 'power breakfasts' I used to have while working as a market researcher in London. Those breakfasts were the playing fields for games of one-up-man-ship (and it usually was a man although women were not necessarily immune), to have breakfast with clients to prove how busy one is, to go to the Savoy, it being the place to see and be seen, to boast about how one doesn't normally have breakfast (too busy) while consuming vast quantities of greasy fried food that gave one indigestion for the rest of the morning. And so on…….

I think what happened in that village 'hotel' was a power breakfast of a different sort. Not the power of being one up on everyone else, but of being shown something that somehow resonated with my internal power, my internal light or flame. Something that accentuated my need to continue to try and respond to the call of the land. It enabled me to go back to the work with renewed energy and hope.

******

We were offered some chickens and decided to take them. Like me, the forty or so birds had had a somewhat chequered history. They had been purchased by someone who then couldn't look after them because of other commitments. They were then passed on to someone else and when he found he couldn't care for them they were offered to me. The integrated chicken project was still being built but we had another place where we could put them and I was pleased to have chickens again. They laid eggs and it was good to have our own source of manure for the compost heaps.

******

The first few days of March found the weather changing from cool to hot – all in a few days – and this at the same time as the fence around the new land was completed. I had decided with Kent that one of the things I should do sooner rather than later was to get rid of all the eucalyptus trees which covered much of the new land. Eucalyptus trees greedily suck up all the available water, as well as put something into the soil which makes it difficult for other trees to grow next to them. I had hoped that I might be able to plants new trees among the eucalyptus and gradually take the eucalyptus away as the new trees got bigger but Kent said this wouldn't work. He thought that the longer they stayed there the worse it would be for the soil and that they would have to be cleared completely before I could grow anything else.

In the beginning I had had a group of men come and do tree removal with simple tools, but now it seemed the same job could be done much quicker and easier with a recently acquired bulldozer. It duly turned up with its very proud owner/driver one morning with the assurance that all the trees could be taken out and cleared by the end of the day. The machine was very noisy and a backdrop to our work all that day and into the evening. What was much worse than the noise of the machine was the tearing sound as the trees were ripped out of the earth. It felt so violent and the devastation of the soil laid bare was terrible, but somehow necessary. The wood and roots were taken away and the last job the bulldozer did was to level the ground. This conveniently did all the bunding for us but at the cost of disturbing all the topsoil, most of which went into the bunds.

Sitting in what looked like a desert I had very mixed feelings about what I had done. Had such drastic surgery really been necessary? It looked very bare and dusty and I wished it hadn't had to be quite so brutal. A few days later, at the Spring Equinox which is also Earth Day, we had our first meditation at the stones of the sacred circle and my book about the first year in Buddha Garden was published.

EARTH DAY MEDITATION

I look back and see this land as it once was, covered with forest. An uninterrupted mass of green. A place where elephants and tigers roam. A forest, only three or four metres high, but with a profusion of trees, bushes, vines and lianas that form a dense and sometimes impenetrable undergrowth.

I see the first trees being felled close to the city to drive away the tigers. In the following years more trees are cut to provide wood for building. I see the land gradually becoming exposed to the elements especially when plots are given to anyone who will clear and cultivate it for a year. I see the last remaining pieces of forest being cut down fifty years ago to make boats.

In less than two hundred years what was once green and fertile has been turned into an expanse of baked red earth scarred with gullies and ravines. In the monsoon rain the earth bleeds as red topsoil is swept into the sea.

In this desert local people continue to try and grow food. On the land where I have made a vegetable garden a family grows ragi and sorghum, but often there are empty bellies and hunger when the rains don't come. Years later things seem to improve when chemical fertilizers and pesticides like DDT are used. But as time goes by the land gives less and less and earning money to buy food is much easier. The family plants eucalyptus on their land. It needs very little care yet provides cash as the trees are cut to grow and grow again, taking up any remaining nutrients in the soil.

I come to this land to grow food – for myself and for the community. I come to this land to feel the living pulse of the earth, to create a place where I can focus, where I can dream, where I can create.

BECOMING

*I give this place my blessing and pray that its wounds may be healed and it
be restored to life, as
I too may be healed and restored.*

******

The new large water tank for the garden was installed and it was good to have more control over this resource. At least we could measure how much water we put on the beds and could pump at any time of the day. Unfortunately we then started having water problems for other reasons. As it got hotter and drier the water level in the well got lower and was sometimes pumped dry. Water was also being sold to a builder to help the difficult financial situation in Siddhartha Farm. As a result we barely had enough water for the vegetable garden and nothing left over for anything else. The extra compost we had made for the fruit and cashew trees to be planted during the summer rains couldn't be watered enough and so didn't decompose properly.

Since the builders were already working with us we decided to have a few extra jobs completed. We decided to install underground pipes for the cow urine system. The very long hoses that we had been using were so difficult to use that often we never got round to doing the job and the plants suffered accordingly. With more space I decided it would be good to have our own volunteer accommodation and this was built in the form of capsules which, being built with all natural materials and thatched with keet (woven coconut leaves), were very comfortable for this climate. I began to think of Buddha Garden as Buddha Garden Community Farm – a place where people from within and without Auroville could come and experience what it meant to farm organically and live lightly on the land.

That was for the future and in the present it seemed that most of my day, when the morning work was finished, consisted of focusing on the building work. Every day I made 'to do' lists which seemed to get longer and longer as it got hotter and hotter.

Finish bathroom and toilet for volunteers
Make healing garden
Make rotation yards for chickens
Clean everything under my capsule
Make two capsules with doors for volunteers
Make horse corral and drinker (this for my youngest daughter)
Do water system including system for orchard

Make portable drip system for rotation yards
Make underground cow urine system
Tiles and whitewash for Rachael's room and kitchen

Garden work ready for hot season

Plant all the snake gourd
Plant sweet potato on back bed
Clear up back beds
Put up sticks and string for snake gourds
Look at and repair drip system
Collect organic material and make compost for orchard and cashew plantation
Order fruit and cashew trees

There was also the problem of the granite pillars with which I had planned to build the fence around the three rotation yards next to the chicken house. Annoyingly there were no granite pillars to be had because of some dispute between quarry owners and lorry drivers. Since there seemed no end in sight to the dispute and I wanted to get the rotation yards finished, we looked for other ways of doing it. After a lot of discussion we decided to use metal posts which, although somewhat more expensive, were much easier to deal with, being lighter than granite, and able to stand up to the weather very well.

I had started to breed more chickens from our original group, but decided that I would like to be rather more systematic with chickens of a more reliable strain. Together with another farmer we therefore decided to buy a small number of chickens from a chicken breeder with the intention of breeding our own. Unfortunately this did not work at all. From the very beginning they did not seem very strong with legs that looked rather long for the size of their bodies, and even the latter seemed rather too large for their age. I wondered if they had been given growth hormones and grown too quickly. Whether it was that or the stress of the long journey from Chennai, one by one they started to sicken and die until after a few weeks only half of them were still alive. The same thing had happened with the group sent to the other farmer so we decided to put the two groups together on his farm although whether it was a good idea to try to breed from such obviously weak chickens was debatable. Maybe the increasing heat wasn't helping although we tried to keep them as cool as we could, putting their pen under a shady tree and covering them with mats during the heat of the day.

We couldn't find any other chickens anywhere so once the chicken project buildings were finished we started by moving our original group into the new quarters. This was somewhat depleted now we had got rid of most of the cockerels who had seemed to spend their whole time noisily fighting and I was sure were stopping the hens from laying. Without them the whole place felt much more calm, although egg production did not rise as I had hoped. Maybe that was because they were moved at about the same time or maybe because it was getting hotter. It was difficult to say.

******

Then it seemed that nature rebelled. One very hot afternoon during a very hot May my watchman came running to me 'come quick, come quick, all the chickens are dying' and it was true they were literally keeling over one by one in the heat. By the time I got there six had already died one after the other and it looked as if others might follow. We quickly got the hose and sprayed the house with water on the outside as well as putting leaves on top of it. We then soaked their bedding which wouldn't have been such a good idea at any other time but at that point helped them to cool down. We put a tarpaulin over the large run to create more shade and eventually I got a shade net.

Only a few days later we had the most terrible storm. It lasted for only about forty minutes but in that time it destroyed the roof on top of the storeroom. The roof shifted sideways and took some masonry with it. It also blew down one of the capsules which was nearly finished – the granite pillars were shattered. The roof on the new chicken house holding up the net was also very twisted. Before the storm I had been seeing the building work as almost finished and was hoping for a few weeks of quiet without the builders before the summer rains started and with it the more intense work in the garden. Then this happened and I felt absolutely devastated. It felt as if everything I had struggled for over the previous months had been cancelled in just a few minutes of nature's fury.

Watching the roof being removed so that the building could be repaired I felt unutterably tired. I didn't feel like doing anything and often found myself in a daze playing computer games for what felt like hours. I felt heavy and miserable, battered by all the problems that I'd experienced over the previous months relating to the people, the land and nature. So much work completely wiped out by natural phenomena which came like a bolt of lightening and with the same effect.

That was how my second year on the land came to a close.

******

The summer months of April to June had felt very long and very hot and I don't think I always appreciated how much energy it took to cope with the extra work of building as well as keeping on top of all the garden work in the increasing heat. I felt as if I hadn't had a chance to slow down – in fact I felt I had been made to go faster than was really good for me with the increase in the pace of building work being matched by the increasing heat. I kept planning that once a certain number of jobs were finished then I would take a break. Arjunan had taken two weeks off to go to Bangalore on the understanding that he would look after the place when he returned. But when he came back I was immersed in all the building work necessary to make good the damage caused by the storm as well as trying to finish off things for our first residential volunteer who had booked to come in June.

He turned up unexpectedly early and although everything didn't feel quite ready, he was ready to be flexible and put up with the not quite finished condition of the facilities. He was a willing worker who I enjoyed having around. It gave me a taste of things to come and the various things I needed to organise better if volunteers were to get the most out of their experience in Buddha Garden.

I could feel the new season starting with the first heavy rain which came in mid-June and I started to feel more optimisitc. The dry land sucked it up and watching the rain fall I hoped this time would be a time of renewal for me as well as the land. Unlike the previous summer we had not cancelled the mixed bags although there were very few during this hot season as this is the time when many people leave Auroville to go to the west. There was so little coming out of the garden and yet miraculously there always seemed to be something which was more or less enough for those who wanted it. It was wonderful how things were still coming given that it had been so hot and the plants looked as yellow and exhausted as I felt.

Becoming

At the summer solstice I felt I had got over some sort of hump in terms of finishing the building work. With the first rains the land seemed to become more alive and with it came the need for a lot of work directly with the land.

> *The monsoon rain*
> *Has come at last*
> *Drenching the dry earth*
> *And my dry heart.*
>
> *A wet benediction*
> *And promise*
> *Of new beginnings?*

I felt very tired and often didn't feel so much enthusiasm for this work although at the same time it was also exciting to see the development of the farm. Now was the time when many of the different parts were in place and I could start to see how the energies might balance and support each other as Kent and I had talked about so many months previously. But how to do it in for myself? I thought that if I really saw my life and how I was living it at that time I would find it quite unsupportable. Sometimes I wondered how I could go on with the relentlessness of the work and the continuing problems that were the backdrop to everything that we were doing.

Starting work in the beautiful mornings helped. With the sun rising and a gentle breeze it was often a time when I felt calm enough to really feel the energy in the garden – and to feel that it was sustaining me. It was also good having more volunteers living in Buddha Garden despite the fact that it did take up quite a lot of my time and attention. We seemed to get so much work done in the midst of such positive and vigorous vibrations. Hard work like clearing a heavily weed infested bed felt so much lighter when there were willing hands to not only help with doing it but also to feel interested in the result. With a willing group of workers it was a really enjoyable experience and such times reminded me of what fun it could be when there was a group and the work just flowed and we all enjoyed ourselves together.

******

When the rains began in earnest in August I realized that the work of planting flowed much more easily in this third year. With the nursery and the use of nets most of the beds were now completely full with plants which, because of the work we had done with composting the beds, were green and glossy and healthy and much less liable to be attacked by pests.

But once again, while one part of the work seemed to be coming along well I suffered more stealing and vandalism. I felt that I had done what I could to ameliorate the situation yet despite this it only needed the slightest relaxation – in one case the watchman being off sick for two days – and it all started happening again. One night I went into the chicken yard to find that a third of the chickens were missing. Someone had made a hole in both outer perimeter fence and chicken fence and had managed to crawl in and taken them away.

I felt as if I had worked and worked for nothing. Perhaps it was too much to expect that the local people could understand or appreciate what I was doing and not see me only as a source of things to come and take. Sometimes it seemed too difficult to carry on. There were an increasing number of days when I felt lost at heart, a sort of empty feeling that deepened my resolution of not wanting to do the work or be in Buddha Garden anymore. I didn't want to have to get up every morning and be responsible for all the things that needed doing. I didn't want to be the person to move the energy that made things change, the person that had to make all the plans or who had to start the ball rolling if the plans were to become a reality. I didn't want to be the anchor, the person who was deeply enmeshed in the place and to whom everyone came to looking for direction and support.

In such a situation it was only possible to carry on if I had a light within to sustain me, but at that time I felt as if this had been snuffed out – or at least considerably dimmed by the recent spate of stealing. How could I carry on? The future looked so very bleak when it seemed that whatever positive things I managed to create would not only be unappreciated but stolen or destroyed either by people or by a quirk of nature.

I walk through filthy sludge
Which was once sacred earth

Step by arduous step, lifting
My sinking feet from
A squelching mire.

The next step is all there is.

I did not see how I could carry on in Buddha Garden and yet every morning I did get up as the sun rose. I did do the work that was needed…

******

That year, although there was some rain it was overall somewhat dry and we had to wait longer than usual for the really heavy rains which would soak the earth and make tree planting possible. As soon as the earth was soft enough we employed a group of diggers to come and dig holes for the trees and the earth bunds that would stop the water running off the land and keep the top soil from washing away. In the meantime we were able to plant the cashew trees that we had been nurturing in the nursery ever since the hot weather began, the original nuts coming from a special tree in Auroville.

We intended to plant the trees on the area that had been bulldozed by the digger. Since it still looked very bare we decided to first plant it with nitrogen fixing green manure before planting the trees. This involved getting a tractor to do the ploughing and then all rushing out when the soil was wet to scatter the seeds. We started in a long line at one end and threw the seed around until we had finished it. We then got the seeds covered using a local type of harrow made of woven branches and pulled by bullocks. After that the holes were dug and on another wet day we planted the cashew trees, covering them with palmyra leaves to protect them from the sun which still seemed very hot despite the rain.

We waited anxiously for more rain so that we could plant the forest trees and eventually it did come. At the time there were a group of young people working regularly in Buddha Garden, some of them staying on the farm and others coming regularly on a daily basis. On a very grey day when everything was wet and drippy and muddy we started planting the trees for the forest. We all worked really hard knowing that the sooner we got them in the more they would have of the monsoon rain and the more likely they were to grow. On the first day we completed two large sections of planting and it looked absolutely wonderful to see the green plants on what before had looked like a bare moonscape.

A satisfying aspect of the job was that, unlike growing vegetables, planting trees wouldn't have to be done again. 'All' they had to do was grow. They were tough local trees that could survive the harsh climate and since we had given them a good start with a hole filled with compost, we felt that they had a good chance. I thought we had also caught the moment in terms of putting them in at a time when they would have the maximum of monsoon rain. With such a large and energetic group of us doing the work it felt as if the planting got done more or less effortlessly. It was a wonderful morning of working together and I felt that we had blessed the garden which was in turn blessing us.

Why was it that such a positive experience could be followed that same night with vandalism and destruction of our work? We had another break in where two huge holes were made in the back fence and someone had come in and pulled up all the trees in two sections where we had planted. I felt SO tired and disheartened but realized I just had to carry on otherwise everything would not be in place when the monsoon started properly and we would have missed an important growing period for that year. Feeling hopeless, I helped with everyone else to replant the trees once again as well as completing planting the forest, the living fence and the wood lot right at the furthest extent of the land.

During this period we had another huge thunderstorm which came frighteningly overhead at one point. The resulting torrents of water washed away some of the earth bunds which showed that the bunding hadn't been put in quite correctly. It was difficult to see exactly where the mistakes were without going out while it was raining and watching how the water flowed. Since the storm was directly over head and in the middle of the night I didn't much fancy doing this. Somehow this destruction didn't seem so bad when the next morning we worked together to repair the bunds and enjoyed ourselves tremendously getting wet and muddy in the process.

We finished the tree planting with the planting of a ceremonial tree on Diwali which is the Indian festival of light. I wished that I could feel more light inside me.

DIWALI PRAYER

I lay myself down upon the ground.
Upon this earth with which we have
Labored so long to bring to life.

I ask that the rain may come and
With the sun nurture the new life
In these young seedlings.

As the earth transforms, I ask
That I too, may be renewed.

******

As the year came to an end in December the work of creating the farm also came to a close. Now our work was to harness and integrate the different energies of the land which would enable us to produce more food. This was the time, when I felt that Buddha Garden should become independent of Siddhartha Farm and be a farm in its own right. I wrote how I thought it should become a community farm. A place where others could come and experience something about growing food and living lightly on the land. A place of experiential education where we would learn and hopefully transform together.

Once again at a time when I thought I should feel elated I felt extremely tired and very empty. I also felt very vulnerable as the stealing continued and it seemed to me that given this had happened so many times I should by now have found a more positive and less energy-draining way of dealing with it. Once more I thought about my choice to work on the land. Once more I tried to see what the situation could teach me.

I began by trying yet again to clarify the nature of the choice I had made, and continued to make, seemingly in the teeth of a lot of difficulties. I started off doing what many self-help books tell you to do which is to make lists of 'positives' and 'negatives' regarding the situation. I am sure it is very helpful in some situations but in this case I soon found that it wasn't very relevant. It reminded me of the time long ago when I became pregnant by accident and had to decide whether to have an abortion or not. I made a very long list of reasons why I did not want another baby. But this list was eclipsed by the deep feeling I had, supported by dreams and being in a caring relationship with Peter, that I should have this baby.

I felt similarly about being in Buddha Garden. On the face of it my decision to come here was ridiculous; there being far more negative than positive reasons on every level. There were a lot of practical problems ranging from the poor soil and difficult climate as well as personal problems with various individuals. Emotionally I felt I was in a wasteland having total responsibility on my own when I would much rather do the work as part of a group. Also, in being the anchor who had to provide the energy to start anything happening, I felt was a very heavy and sometimes stressful responsibility, which limited my options in many ways – from being unable to go away for a holiday to having little or no time for other activities in

Auroville. I could not think of a practical or 'lifestyle' reason as to why I should do this work except that I liked living close to nature, but I could have done this in a much less difficult situation, even in Auroville.

But no. As with the decision to have a child rather than an abortion, the negative reasons were eclipsed by a deeper movement that somehow made Buddha garden the right place for me at that time. That it was a place for me to move forward with my inner learning. And that however difficult this might be, the practical problems were either not very significant or were an important part of the learning process. I also felt a vibration with the place, with the land, that being here in some way amplified a vibration within myself which allowed me to become more myself, however that might be.

One thing I considered was whether I was reinventing the situation of my difficult birth in order to feel more alive. I know that many times during my life I have done this when I have taken action to upset an 'easy' situation to make it more challenging and myself feel more energized. There was also the fear that if I were not struggling then I may not survive. I supposed there might have been an element of this although I was very aware of how the challenges of this situation usually did lead to my learning something about myself.

In any case I was clear that I was not prepared to carry on in an open-ended way. I decided that if things did not change substantially by the time Buddha Garden had been established – when it had become a viable farm – then I would think seriously about leaving. This future decision, however, would of course depend on what happened as when the time came I might find that the elements of the situation which I found so difficult as I wrote this may have lost their intensity and become irrelevant. So yes, I saw I wanted a challenge but not just a difficult life for the sake of it being difficult so that I felt more alive.

I knew I had made a demanding choice deciding to engage with the earth in the way that I did. Gradually I had become aware that I was not just making a pretty place or growing vegetables only for myself. I was growing vegetables and producing eggs for everyone in the community. This required a certain amount of consistent work every day as well as keeping in touch with what was going on with the land outside of the normal working hours. There is a responsibility about farming which is not there in most other sorts of jobs. I felt very much like an anchor which did constrain my movements. There were also many things over which I did not have any control; the most important one being the weather.

Another reason I thought I might be in Buddha Garden was that in engaging with the earth to grow food, I was embodying in the external world something that I want to happen internally. That what I was doing externally resonated with what was happening internally. Although how the nature of these connections worked, continued to be unclear.

The other element of this choice – and certain other similar choices I had made in my life – was that although there was definitely an option I felt there was only one path to be taken. I suppose the first time I felt this strongly and was able to articulate it was when I was at that first farm in the Valley. So many things seemed to be wrong for me and yet I felt very strongly that this was the place where it was right for me to be. It was a peculiar and rather mysterious feeling knowing that if I wanted to I could choose something else, but at the same time knowing that really there was only one choice to be made. The only way I can describe it is that there was a deep feeling of rightness about the choice despite the negative consequences that it might bring.

I felt that such a choice required a deep trust in the process of life and that I would be drawn to places and people that were necessary for me to grow and move on. That while I was in whatever situation was right for me, I would have the necessary support on all levels that I needed to learn from it, even if it didn't feel like that.

Perhaps it was this trust I was lacking....

DIALOGUE
Dreams told me
'Feed the earth'

'How?' I replied

Crying dry tears
Of exhaustion
Under the sun.

'Easy!' She said

'Become water
and overflow'

How I Grew With My Garden

******

At the beginning of the new year, although everything for the farm was now in place I was finding the day-to-day running of the farm increasingly difficult. Getting up to start work in the morning was a daily challenge. It was around this time and for most of the next year that I was faced with a situation that I had never had to face before – a situation of feeling actively undermined in what I was doing. A situation that drained the very last dregs of energy out of me.

In all the time that I had been in Buddha Garden I had never felt very supported by the community of Auroville. This was intensified by having to deal with most of the practical difficulties alone as well as my personal feelings of isolation and loneliness. This time, however, it seemed that I was being actively undermined, by a group within the community as well as by individuals living close to Buddha Garden.

One strand of the process had begun the previous year when a local group had come to Auroville demanding land for a women's handicraft project. The money was going to be provided by the Government to build a centre where women doing craft work could bring their produce to be sold. This had to built on government or 'peremboke' land and the project holders wanted to build where they could take advantage of the large numbers of people coming to see Auroville and particularly Matrimandir. There was a small piece of Government land opposite to Matrimandir on which they hoped to build.

Since Matrimandir is considered to be the spiritual center of Auroville, such a commercial project was considered unacceptable and therefore, hastily refused, leading to a frantic search for another suitable piece of land in a better location. The hurry was partly because of constraints about the money which had to be given before the end of the financial year and would only be given if a suitable plot of land was made available. Various plots of land within Auroville were extended and refused as either being the wrong size or in the wrong place. Then they looked at the field in the front of Siddhartha Farm and it seemed that this would be ideal in many ways. It was the right size and on the approach road to the Visitors Centre and therefore available to all the passing traffic into Auroville. I was not very keen on having this building at the front of the farm but was told that because resolving this state of affairs was necessary for the greater good of Auroville, both Herbert and I should agree to it.

Reluctantly I did so as one thing that bothered me was that although it was supposed to help poor women I had not seen one woman involved. I was also worried about where the water would come from - I did not want our dwindling supplies of water to go towards yet more construction - and I was also concerned about rubbish disposal. Having seen the mess on some local building sites I wanted to avoid that if possible. There was also the problem that the concerned piece of land carried our access path from the tar road to the farm so that another access path would need to be found and made. I raised all these queries but was assured that this was going to be a joint Auroville/village project and there would be a group who would resolve such matters. With that assurance Herbert and I didn't feel we had much choice but to agree to the land being used for this purpose.

For the next six months there were various problems that took enormous amounts of energy to resolve as there was no steering group as promised and it seemed very unclear as to who was in charge and had authority. Whenever there was a problem to be solved it was always someone else's responsibility – usually someone that it was more or less impossible to get to see because he was so busy. When they dug the foundations for the building and the path was dug up, the telephone cable got cut yet again. At the same time they made us a new path by the side of the project across open village land, but this enraged people in the village as they felt that they should have been asked to give their permission. As a result a deputation from the village came to Herbert and said that we could not use the new path – although eventually we came to the agreement that we would not make the path official by either working on it or laying the telephone cable. This meant that for the next few months our telephone relied on a flimsy temporary cable going through the trees. The line was, however, cut on several occasions when heavy machinery was brought in to do various building jobs on site.

Trying to come to some agreement about the new path required participation in endless meetings with village and Auroville individuals, none of which seemed able to resolve the situation. Increasingly I felt that I had been lied to, and that all anyone in Auroville wanted was the land so they could resolve a difficult situation. Once that had been achieved everyone seemed to lose interest although to be fair one or two individuals did do their best to try and help solve the subsequent problems. In the village this situation activated other resentments about their treatment by Auroville so all that had to be discussed as well.

As the situation deteriorated I became very upset by the bitterness I had started to feel and express to the group involved. I could see it was quite pointless in terms of achieving anything, even as I made these expressions. I was told that 'we all have to do what is necessary to solve the problem and put aside all the past and the emotional feelings we have about the situation' – which was all very well but I didn't feel I had the inner strength to do so. I felt like shouting and screaming and crying so that everyone could see how badly I had been treated. I could also see that the bitterness was very corrosive. It affected me more than them and it was within me that it somehow had to be resolved. At such times I did not think my inner work had gone very far or very deep.

******

Another upsetting situation that totally undermined my efforts concerned the person who had come to live in my house in Siddhartha Forest after I had moved out. He had come to me with his family and told me how he had been in Auroville for some time and how much he wanted to become Aurovilian. They could not do so until they had found a permanent place to live rather than the guest house where they had been living for some time. As a local person with a family I understood how he hadn't been able to raise enough money to pay for my house, the proceeds of which would automatically be used in Buddha Garden. Could they pay over a period of time? He told me that it was very likely that he would be getting money from the Government for a project and that from this regular income he would be able to give me the money for the house. So on that understanding he and his family moved in.

Then, over a period of time, it seemed there were various problems. He became very violent with the other community members and it became clear that he had been corrupt in his use of the project money, using it to buy land for himself rather than for the purposes to which he had said it would be used. When this eventually came to light and the whole situation was being discussed with various groups in Auroville he told them that he had no intention of giving me money for the house. 'It's a group asset and why should I have to pay for that?' was his reasoning. As a result I felt exploited and manipulated. I had let him have the house in good faith on what was basically an extended loan from my own pocket and with that he had taken advantage of my good will.

The third strand of the undermining process happened when I found out quite by chance that Herbert had ploughed up and planted with casuarinas a plot of land at the edge of Buddha Garden. I had talked about maybe expanding onto this land in the future to grow rice. I felt that by his actions Herbert was trying to stop me doing this as casuarinas trees take some years before they can be harvested, effectively blocking any further development of the land.

Each of these things happened on a different side of Buddha Garden and I felt that I was being squeezed between them all.

****

This general situation was epitomized for me one Sunday when a group of local men came to cut down trees on the village land just beyond my fence. Instead of cutting the trees in a way that made the trees fall away from the fence they let them fall on the fence and break it. When I remonstrated with them the leader threatened me with his knife.

I looked at the fence which had cost me so much - and not only in money - to build. I saw yet one more thing I had tried to create, being destroyed, and having to be mended. This had happened so many times since I set up Buddha Garden that I had lost count. It seemed that every time I had tried to create something then it was destroyed either by human or natural agency. Is this the way of creation? If it carried on like this I felt that I would never be able to create a secure base in Buddha Garden.

The fact that it was suddenly so draining worried me a lot. Each time I had experienced such problems I tried to deal with them positively, and since I had arrived in Buddha Garden felt that I was slowly getting better at doing this. I told myself that each time I resolved a difficult situation I could also use it as an opportunity for me to establish the right energy needed here just a little bit more. At the same time, however, I felt I had got to the point where each time I was asked to deal with yet another element of destruction or undermining I was getting a little more drained. I didn't seem to be able to find a way of renewing myself. At one level I thought this was because there was no one to help me share the responsibilities but at a deeper level it felt like something else – that even the Divine force was not supporting me.

When life was such a battlefield I felt as if I must be doing something wrong. I was so tired of having to fight all the time, and being forced to accept the destruction which seemed to be part and parcel of anything that I created. Surely there was more to the work than this, wasn't there? Or perhaps dealing with this was the real work? When all was said and done I didn't feel that I was really creating anything very much when it all seemed so fragile and easily dismantled. Was the real work something to do with dealing with this seemingly unending process of creation/destruction which was so draining but might eventually end up with something gained?

I could not see how to get out of this impasse. I mustered my energies and dealt with each problem as positively as I could in a situation where I felt very little support, love or appreciation. Perhaps there wasn't anything I could do except carry on with the trust that things would eventually change when the time was right. Perhaps I needed to love and appreciate myself more for what I had managed to accomplish. Despite everything, Buddha Garden did exist.

In March I had a series of dreams that seemed to be saying that I should be changing my focus. That I should focus more internally to support the creative part of myself – allowing and protecting the creative process. This came at a time when I felt that I had very little energy and didn't feel like writing although I did continue to do a little painting. Like the place, I felt squeezed on all sides.

******

With the feeling of my energy dripping away each time I had a problem to solve I was very aware that I was not being renewed especially at deeper levels. I felt as if all my energies were going towards holding myself together and that there was very little indeed left over for expressing myself. I felt as if I were in a vacuum, with only what I could muster from my internal energies being there to support me – and that these were under severe stress at the time. For many reasons I was feeling extremely insecure and undermined and was beginning to wonder whether Auroville was really my place. Was I undermining myself by staying in what seemed to be such a bleak situation?

This was not of course a very productive way of responding, as whether Auroville was my place or not would become evident in the fullness of time. I didn't think this was a problem I could 'think through' and come to a decision about, but was more something that I needed to feel with my heart and to see where that led. I had tried, and failed, to find that place within where no one could undermine me. Soon, quite by chance, I came across the following quotation – another instance when I felt Mother speaking to me:

> 'Those that stay here (in Auroville) know that for them there is no other place in the world they could be. If that inner certitude is not with you then do what you must. I will always be one with you in your aspiration………'

As I read it I felt very clearly that I did not have that inner certitude at that time – and I did know what it felt like as I had experienced it before. Perhaps the problem was that I was not a devotee of either Mother or Sri Aurobindo, perhaps devotees would be able to deal with all the setbacks more easily. I knew that it was not a requirement of being in Auroville to be a devotee but perhaps, practically speaking, this was necessary.

Many times I asked the question – is this still my place? But unlike every other time when I had asked this question there was no clear reply.

It was a very low point.

PART FOUR

QUIESCENCE

DEPARTURE AND RETURN

For some months I had been talking to John about Buddha Garden. He had come to Auroville a year or so previously and had been managing another Auroville farm, but wanted a change. So I suggested that he might like to consider coming to help me. Despite being somewhat ambivalent about continuing to run a farm – after thirty years of managing large farms in the west he felt he wanted to do something different, he said he would give it a try, initially for three months.

I was very pleased that at last there was someone who was willing to help me with the work on a more long term basis although I had somewhat mixed feelings about John. He was obviously an excellent farmer but he wasn't sure what he really wanted to do and although he said he didn't mind working with volunteers it was clear that he didn't find this part of Buddha Garden's activities very interesting. Practically I felt sure that we could work together but I didn't feel that we shared the vision. I hoped that maybe he would eventually grow into the place and share the dream with me, but this was not to be.

To make enough space for John more building was required so I built two extra capsules with a bathroom and toilet. Rachael moved to the rebuilt room on top of the store room, and I went to the capsule in the orchard and together we took over what used to be the volunteer kitchen and bathroom by the store room. This left the larger kitchen for volunteers and John took over the room vacated by Rachael for his computer as well as one of the new capsules in which to sleep. Once again there was the stress of moving yet again although once I did so I enjoyed living less in the middle of the farm and more tucked away in my capsule in the orchard.

******

John brought with him a new impetus to the practical work in Buddha Garden and began by taking measures to use the decreasingly available water more efficiently. Rather than spread the water thinly all over the garden as I was then doing, he suggested watering a few beds more intensively. This would make the beds damp all over and provide more nutrients for the plants. They, in turn, would be able to reach further by spreading their roots all over the bed rather than just within the small amount of wet soil around the drippers.

We began the necessary changes on half the beds in the garden putting in new drip lines with drippers closer together and putting three lines on each bed instead of two. With the beds being wetter, the weeding was much easier and we didn't have to water the beds prior to weeding as we had been doing. I was incredulous when, with this new regime, we found we were able to grow twice as much produce on half the number of beds. And this was during the very hot weather when normally the amounts we had been able to produce were negligible.

We therefore decided that we would slowly change all the irrigation pipes – which had been second-hand when we got them and were showing their age. Many of the drip holes had got blocked and because of their design it was difficult to clear them. The lines had many places where they were held together with insulation tape to cover up large holes made by animals in search of water. The new drip lines were made of thicker material and were therefore more animal proof, and the drips were the kind that could be taken apart and cleaned if they got blocked. I realized how in some ways I had been very thoughtless, forging ahead regardless and complaining about the lack of water but doing nothing to use what we had more effectively.

John also did a lot of work in the rotation yards which, although being utilized a little, were not being worked as envisaged. The worst problem was once again the irrigation system which I had cobbled together using bits of old hoses and drip lines as at the time we didn't have the money for anything better. John said we needed a proper system and thought that in these yards we should have sprinklers rather than drippers. There are some plants that don't like water on their leaves, but we had enough beds with drippers for those. For the rest, sprinklers would be suitable and much less expensive than drippers. John had already put in such a system elsewhere and thus knew where to get all the components and how to put them together, so I was pleased to let him and Arjunan get on with it.

******

The practical work was much easier when there were three of us to discuss and then decide the best way of completing the work. John, however, was very much the loner and often seemed to prefer doing things on his own. Although I had told him that working with volunteers was part of the job, he didn't seem to take it to heart. He would walk off on his own to do something when volunteers were obviously waiting for someone to tell them how they could help. I would call after him and when I pointed to the people waiting for a job he would often look very quizzical – as if he had forgotten that we had volunteers. And although he would take them along he didn't always communicate with them very well. They would come back to me to ask what John wanted them to do.

John also had a much more lackadaisical approach than myself to what happened in the kitchen and this seemed to infect the volunteers – or maybe it was just that we had a particularly messy group at that time. One morning I went into the kitchen and found the sink overflowing with dirty plates and cups. I was very annoyed and although eventually I got one of the volunteers to do it, what I really hated was having to point out the situation and then get behind someone to get the job done. I hated being forced into that position. I didn't want to be Big Mummy and a lot of the time that's how I started to feel. It wasn't something I had felt to any great degree before John had arrived.

I was also unhappy with the way everyone came in and sat and talked for half an hour before starting work, often over cups of tea and coffee. It was such a waste of the early morning coolness, especially when later everyone would begin complaining that it was too hot to continue working. Again I felt pushed into the role of making sure that we started work at a reasonable time so that the work didn't suffer. It felt like pushing the mountain especially as John didn't seem to feel any urgency either. Of course the volunteers were there on a holiday or at least taking a break from their ordinary lives. There was no urgency about the work for them and it was no concern of theirs if the farm was not financially viable. They had come to Buddha Garden for an experience and the responsibilities for the farm quite rightly belonged elsewhere.

I began to find dealing with the volunteers more and more exhausting although this was because of how I was feeling rather than there being anything wrong with them. I seemed to have much less patience in answering their questions or in telling them about Buddha Garden when they first arrived. I got to the point where I started to dread it if a volunteer came up to me because I was so afraid that they would be asking for something from me: a solution to a problem or information which required a complicated explanation. It felt as if I were holding the place and everyone in it but that nothing and nobody was holding me. For the volunteers, and for John, Buddha Garden was a stepping stone towards something else. I felt that if there had been a group of people with a shared vision, committed to Buddha Garden, then certain standards and a way of working would have evolved. This would have been apparent to all but the most insensitive of volunteers, who would have seen rather than have to be told about how things were done. As it was I felt I had to remake the community with each individual, explaining the what and how and the why and this in a lot of little ways being at odds with what they actually saw happening.

One of the things I found increasingly irritating was John's heavy smoking. Up to that point smoking had never been much of an issue as I had told everyone coming to Buddha Garden that I did not like smoking especially during working hours. Since I don't smoke most people abided by that rule and didn't smoke in any of the communal places or while working. John, however, seemed unable to do this and gradually smoked more and more, often smoking while working. Others seemed to pick up on this and it got very difficult indeed to stop anyone smoking either during working hours or in communal places. Increasingly I felt I was the only one who had strong feelings about this. Friends told me that I made too much fuss, but I felt that smoking seemed to lower the general energy level apart from creating a lot of extra mess with piles of cigarette butts everywhere and sometimes being thrown down on the ground. It seemed totally inappropriate to me to smoke while working at growing healthy vegetables.

****

Despite these irritations I enjoyed the long talks that I had with John about the farm and liked getting the benefit of his experience and expertise. As we talked I often felt that my knowledge of farming was not very great – that there was a lot of information out there which I hadn't had time and energy to investigate and use. I often felt that somehow Buddha Garden and the way we worked was more like the garden of an enthusiastic amateur than a real farmer. Sometimes I felt stretched between conflicting demands for a reasonable amount of production, and balancing that with wanting to run the place with volunteers and tune into the deeper rhythms of living and being engaged with the land. I also felt that to become more professional it would probably be necessary to make more of a full-time commitment to the farm, which again I didn't want to do.

Talking about it further I also saw that John's idea of farming was focused entirely on the practical management of how to get maximum production with minimum inputs and he wasn't particularly interested in anything else. I agreed with him entirely that it was necessary to manage the very valuable resources of land as well and effectively as possible, and in the interests of sustainability we needed to be financially viable. I did not, however, think it should be the defining feature by which the farm was to be judged as a success of not. We also thought differently about the volunteers as I continued to want them to do all or most of the work while John wanted to employ a local person, especially for the regular afternoon jobs that at present we were doing. I had very mixed feelings about this as I felt that we were on the way to marginalizing the work of the volunteers, and in any case, my experience of local labour had not been very positive. In the end we took someone on – a person that John had already worked with – and it did make things easier for both of us.

John was keen to branch out into new areas using his extensive farming experience so he was very pleased, when together with a friend he managed to obtain a research grant to carry out an extensive assessment of all the Auroville farms. I agreed to carry out the market side of the research as a way of raising money for the new pump which we had decided to have installed. The water problems had continued and we decided that the only way to solve them was to get our own pump. Siddhartha Farm well had a lot of water but the existing pump wasn't powerful enough to pump enough water for both of us. We applied for a government subsidized solar pumping system and a matching three year loan. The money I would receive for doing the research would cover the first nine months or so of the loan repayment and after that we thought that we should be able to pay for it with the increased income that having the pump would hopefully create.

I also wrote a research proposal, which was not accepted, but which had enabled me to examine again the dream I had for Buddha Garden. I saw that I wanted Buddha Garden to have more of an educational role although whether I had the energy to achieve this was debatable. I had hoped this writing would also help me become clear about whether Auroville was my place or not, but it didn't and I continued to be as unclear as I had ever been. Something it did show me, though, was that it was time for Buddha Garden to become an independent farm as we now had all the necessary elements not only in place but also working. WE had grown beyond being the vegetable garden for Siddhartha farm.

******

Something that I had always planned for Buddha Garden was that we should grow field crops – this on a low lying piece of land that flooded during the monsoon. My initial idea was to grow all our chicken food so that the chickens could have organically grown food and therefore produce organic eggs. Up until John came there had been neither the time nor the resources to do this and if the truth be told it was something I felt some anxiety about.

To grow field crops seemed to require a completely different perspective and very different skills from that of growing vegetables.

Having grown various field crops in the UK, John felt quite at home with doing this in Buddha Garden even although he had never grown rice and *varaigu* before. He also knew how to do things like drive the tractor although for our final ploughing we got someone with a better tractor to come and do it for us. There was a lot of work involved. The ploughing had to be started and this was closely related to when the first rains came, although by the time we had decided to go ahead we were rather late. Most local farmers 'open the ground' with the first ploughing as soon as the first rains have made the soil soft enough to do so. Subsequent ploughing is carried out at least twice more, one of which must be done after three days of rain so the soil is really soft and the ploughing can go deeper.

Since we were rather late starting we didn't have time to grow a green manure but had to put sacks of compost on the field instead. We got this through the local Indian government support for farmers – sacks of dried organic compost which we then had to sprinkle all over the field. It didn't seem very much for the size of the field but we hoped that as the fields hadn't had anything grown on them for some time then there might be some residual fertility. Then we had to scatter the seeds and we all found this extremely difficult to do evenly – there is obviously a special knack to it. We hoped that the subsequent harrowing we did would spread them around but when the seeds came up it was clear this hadn't happened as the plants were spread over the field very unevenly.

The fields of red rice and *varaigu* came up quite well but the field of *kambu* had large bare patches after getting flooded during a large rain when a bund was breached. All these crops had to be weeded which was a three-to-four-week backbreaking job for a group of women from the village. Watching them work I didn't see how I could grow these crops just using volunteers. They would not have been able to put in the necessary hours of weeding which has to be done quickly if the weeds are not to gain the upper hand. I loved the vibrant green that these fields became and it was good to see this last part of the farm under cultivation at last.

I couldn't help comparing the vibrant green in the fields with the grey and exhaustion that I felt inside me. I felt out of tune with almost everyone I came in contact with, although, of course, this derived from my own low energy levels. I didn't feel that I was working towards something 'better' or 'higher' – or that I was aligned with something that was greater than just my own little concerns and works. As far as Auroville was concerned I felt undermined rather than uplifted and I didn't seem to be able to keep a connection with something – God or the Divine – that was beyond me. Could I be a light unto myself? I felt it had sputtered out a long time ago and I was just an empty shell, carrying things on because that was what I had to do, and I couldn't see any relief in sight.

> *Empty vessel exhausted*
> *Sun burnt and wind dried.*
>
> *At the touch of*
> *Precise steel.*
> *Shattered.*
> *Into shards in the dirt.*
>
> *Infused with water;*
> *Blended with strong hands.*
> *Caressed and shaped*
>
> *Substance renewed.*

Where was the water? Would I have felt better or worse if I had been part of a real community? When I really thought about what was going on – which I tried not to do too much because I felt so depressed about it – the situation felt almost insupportable.

I wrote and wrote and wrote and wrote and sometimes painted. But I still felt blank and nothing seemed to surface. I continued to feel confused.

'I don't know, I don't know, I don't know – again and again and again…'

What was the lesson in all of this? Somehow I couldn't muster the energy to really look at it and see. I felt overwhelmed and crushed by it and down, down, down. Why did everything feel so wrong? It wasn't just about the things that were wrong – however good the situation there was always likely to be some things wrong and some things right. It was the underlying feeling of discontent about where I was and what I was doing that was so disconcerting.

Was it just lack of energy? I had had a long discussion about this with a guest who had come to visit me earlier in the year. She said I looked tired and burnt out and that it was a reminder of her own experiences with starting a rural school in Europe. It had taken her three years of very hard work, in the beginning mostly on her own, to establish the school, and this had totally exhausted her. In the end she had felt forced to leave as she would have had a nervous breakdown if she had tried to carry on. Her leaving created a vacuum within the school into which other people with new ideas had stepped thus creating something else that grew out of the original ideas and organization that she had set up.

She told me that now the school was a true community school run by a small group of committed people which she thought had been made possible only because she left. She felt that as long as she stayed there it would never have changed as she was so identified with the place. She said she loved to go there now when she could just be a part of the process rather than the prime mover responsible for everything that was going on.

I had thought long and hard about this because I could see my own identification with Buddha Garden and how much I permeated every part of what happened there. I still felt passionate about the work and remarkably, the undermining events and other difficulties I had experienced had not changed that. I still didn't know whether I should stay or go. Was leaving the solution? I had thought about it so much, but only in terms of leaving because I couldn't cope, not leaving to create a new dynamic within the development of the farm.

******

Around this time I had a series of dreams which seemed to reiterate the necessity of my focusing more within. That to truly live and be alive I needed to align my external masculine energy with this internal feminine focus rather than using it to resolve all the palpable problems in Buddha Garden.

One after the other these dreams came, one with some beautiful symbolism related to the liver - as something potent to eat that is good for the blood, as an organ that regenerates itself, as an organ that detoxifies the body and, of course, the meaning of 'liver' as an organ but also of an alive person. I also had a flash of a dream when I had found a boat but there wasn't a drop of water anywhere so I couldn't use it to float away. I took this to symbolise that whatever I was seeking was within rather than without.

Did I do anything to facilitate something to allow this change to happen? Mostly I did not as I could not see how I could change things to give myself more time and space. John still needed my help and the needs of the volunteers seemed to require my being there. I took no practical measures to change any of the externals in Buddha Garden although with John it was easier to carry on from day-to-day. I continued to feel the work on the land as ever more therapeutic when I didn't have to organize absolutely everything. As I did the simple garden tasks and could let go of some of the 'must dos,' I could feel it healing and grounding me.

Yet one dream in this series gave me a strong push to collect together some of the writing I had been doing over the previous two years. Miraculously time seemed to become available in which to do this and I made a collection of my poems called 'Desert Footsteps'

> *To make a path in the desert*
> *You must first go there.*
>
> *Then you must stay there, open,*
> *To each and all of its vicissitudes.*
> *Allowing the heart of the desert*
> *To be within you and of you.*
>
> *When you and the desert are deeply*
> *At one, let your feet trace the path*
> *Of this knowing, etching your foot-*
> *Prints into the earth.*
>
> *For all.*

******

Then we were confronted with yet more disturbance when a group of men from the nearby village came and tore down the fence surrounding the rice which had taken so much time and trouble to grow. This piece of land had been sold to Auroville some years previously but the family maintained they had never been paid adequately for a one metre strip of government land down the edge of their field that they had worked on. This often happens. Farmers will plough a little into the government land at the side of their field – perhaps a meter or so as this farmer had done – and plant it. When the land is sold they cannot get any money for this land – it belongs to the

Government – but often they will ask for and be paid a small amount of money in acknowledgement of the work which they have done. Once the land is fenced by Auroville, however, it has to be done along the original lines of the field and cannot include this extra land. This payment by Auroville is thus a goodwill gesture.

The group came one Sunday morning and started tearing the fence down. At that point it was very unclear what the dispute was about. John and I had to rush around trying to contact various people both in the village and in Auroville – almost impossible on a Sunday morning – and ask them to come and help us. Eventually I found someone from the village who managed to persuade the group to stop destroying the fence and agree to come to a meeting to discuss the problem the following day. We managed to put the fence up again but it was very wobbly.

In the following week there were various meetings with groups from the village and within Auroville but the issue wasn't resolved to the family's satisfaction and they came and did the same thing the following weekend. This time with a larger group – obviously this was turning out to be a major attraction for a certain element in the village on Sunday mornings. Once again we managed to stop them but by this time it was clear that the fence would need to be replaced. In the meantime we mended it as best we could but the cows kept knocking it down and getting into the rice which was just at the stage when it was particularly attractive to them – a point obviously not lost on those doing the damage. As a result our worker had to spend a lot of his time just sitting there to make sure that the cows did not get in.

I wept. Once again it seemed that just as we had started something new the forces of destruction came out in strength. The rice which had taken so much effort and money to get this far was slowly getting destroyed before our very eyes. Even with our best efforts the cows still managed to get in and the eventual harvest was much smaller than it should have been.

Ultimately, with the help of various people the problem was resolved although the fence was damaged beyond repair and an expensive new one had to be set up

I felt quite numb.

******

As I tried to respond as positively as I could, and do all the necessary practical things that needed attending, to I could see that I had little or no inner resources of strength and energy left. Even with the help of John. Of all the final straws that I had experienced, this was the ultimate event that gave me the push to start making specific plans to leave Buddha Garden..

It wasn't the first time that John and I had talked about my leaving, but one night I found myself saying very definitely 'I want to move out of Buddha Garden. I want to spend the next six months writing and I want a secluded place away from here where I am free to do that. There are some changes needed here which I don't think will ever happen if I stay. ' All this coming out without any thought from that deeper river within me and me knowing as I said it that this was true. John agreed that he would take over the farm for six months so I could do this.

Having at last come to a sense of rightness I then found that finding another place to live was extremely difficult if not impossible. There were very few houses available, but I made what arrangements I could only to find again and again one after the other, the arrangements falling through. When this had happened several times I began to get very despairing and decided that even if I couldn't leave for six months I would at least take the opportunity to have a break for a week. This was something I hadn't done, apart from the odd weekend, since I had come to Buddha Garden.

******

A week away in another community showed me how practical work could still act as a diversion from my grief and pain. Staying in a place where there were no 'must dos', where I could get up and go to bed any time I felt like it, and where I didn't even have to cook for myself, I found myself consumed by extremely painful feelings. Often the only way I could manage them was to keep myself busy – which in this new place meant writing and painting and finding jobs to do in the kitchen rather than working on the land. I seemed to be in a double bind. I desperately needed to rest from all the doing, but when I did, I got overwhelmed with painful feelings that I found hard to handle except by doing even more.

I have rearranged my life and
Feel for a moment a small
Inner space of relaxation

How I Grew With My Garden

Into which leaps loneliness
Hand in hand with grief
And pain as my back

Burns

I saw that I was burnt out and that I must somehow find a strategy to deal with that as well as the double bind I was in. I saw how perhaps I had got too carried away with expanding the farm so that it had become rather too large for me and, consequently, taken up too much of my time and energy. How it gave me an excuse to work as a diversion to pain and grief. How it also satisfied some childish need to do something useful – this time for Auroville instead of my parents - and therefore be loveable. It was still a challenge to create a situation where I valued my creative self as much as my practical self. In Buddha Garden I had tried to create somewhere and something which would inspire people and where they could come for inspiration and rejuvenation. Except that I hadn't yet learnt how to inspire or rejuvenate myself…
I also realized that a lot of these present feelings of grief had been stirred by my daughter Emma leaving India to live in the UK and go to university there. I missed her.

******

When I came back to Buddha Garden from even this short time away, I felt more lively and it was like a breath of fresh air had blown through the place. John and Arjunan had talked about various ideas and had plans for things that they wanted to implement. This felt like an excellent change. Since it seemed that for the time being I couldn't leave Buddha Garden I decided that I would rearrange things there to have more time for myself. I also planned to have a day, weekend or even a week away on a regular basis. I hoped it would help me feel less desperate about the situation. Maybe things were changing without my having to leave completely.

Unfortunately before any of these new things could happen, John collapsed and had to be taken to hospital. Once again I was totally responsible for everything in Buddha Garden as well as having the extra worry about John although he had other friends who were a great support both to him and to me. He was in hospital for three days and they never did find out exactly what the problem was. He convalesced with friends for the next few weeks and I felt a huge gap. It was lovely to breathe clean air again, but how I missed his practical help. I felt the positive effects of my week's holiday drain away rather quickly.

While John was away, Arjunan told me that he would be leaving soon as well. He had been accepted for a six month internship in Arcosanti, a project in the USA. I was very pleased as over the previous year we had, from time to time, talked about how he might travel to somewhere in the West. We had looked at different possibilities but all of them seemed to be too expensive and/or complicated to arrange. He was going to Arcosanti as a result of two volunteers from that community coming to work in Buddha Garden. They had talked to him about the project and helped him to apply.

I also knew that one of the long-term volunteers, someone who had been in Buddha Garden for nearly a year, was also about to leave.

Once again I felt very alone and couldn't understand why I had another dream showing me the need, yet again, to focus on the inner work. How could I do that when things in the external world were so difficult? When all the people who were giving me the most support were leaving? What was I supposed to do?

******

John returned to Buddha Garden but in the following weeks when Arjunan and then the long-term volunteer left, something seemed to die within me. I gave up. I felt that John didn't really share the vision and I couldn't carry it on my own any longer. I felt there needed to be a group of committed people who shared the vision. They hadn't come and in fact the opposite had happened. I had been assailed from all sides and had kept this vision in the teeth of opposition from many quarters, rather than being supported. I think I had done as much as I could and now didn't want to do so any more.

On the one hand I felt relief at having decided to give up although also very sad that the needed support had not been forthcoming.

Of all deaths
Death of the dream
Is worst

A grey emptiness
Devoid of meaning
And hope.

******

The undermining I had experienced continued to upset me. It wasn't just that I was still dealing with the practical aftermath – it was to be almost a year before the proper telephone cable was restored – but that I was still feeling victimized. Had I failed to protect myself adequately? Thinking about it I felt that I had, yet this undermining had happened, not once, but three times on three different sides of Buddha Garden. Presumably there was some kind of lesson here but I had the greatest difficulty in seeing what it was.

I could perceive that in the past I had often undermined myself by taking on far too much for one person. Even as I got older I had continued to be hopelessly idealistic and ambitious in my vision of what I would be able to achieve in any particular time and place. In Buddha Garden I had not only been unrealistic, I had also beaten myself when things did not turn out as I had hoped – or rather expected. In addition to all this, I had pushed myself to work harder and harder until I had been forced to stop. Maybe this was why I had not attracted anyone – who would be willing to work like that? Keeping Buddha Garden together took almost all my energy, with my painting and writing squeezed into whatever time was left.

Eventually, I came to the conclusion that this was the lesson of the undermining I had experienced and that I needed to be more gentle with myself. I needed to be more realistic and accept my limitations for what they were. Maybe not all was lost. When I had not been able to leave Buddha Garden, I had rearranged my life within the parameters of what was possible, to give myself more time to write and paint. Perhaps at last I was learning to take better care of myself.

******

Having made all these arrangements to stay, it now seemed that my houses in Siddhartha Forest would become vacant after all, as the person occupying them was leaving Auroville. I was wavering about whether I should go back there or not. Jean Marie, who had taken over the responsibility for Siddhartha Forest, wanted me to return but when he first came to talk about it, I told him 'no, I do not want to move back there'. I felt too tired to involve myself with yet another move and more building work and all the disruption that would entail.

Then John decided, that with all the extra work for the Farm Assessment research he not only needed a new computer, but a larger and better space in which to put it. If I moved out this would be possible without doing any extra building. So I thought once again about the houses in Siddhartha Forest which, despite the problems, had many of the qualities that I was looking for. They were in a place where I could be quiet and withdrawn and with the forest, could also feel close to the earth. It was true that I would need a solar system but this was not an insuperable problem as John had spare panels and a battery that he said I could borrow.

With this in mind I went back to Siddhartha Forest for one more look and as I did so, felt the land calling to me. Here was where I had come as a sanctuary after leaving Adventure -- could it be a sanctuary for me again? The previous few months had been very difficult for Jean Marie having to deal with this very tricky person who had been living in my house. He had been both violent and corrupt as well as indulging in various sorts of sexual misbehaviour with local women. The place needed healing as much as myself. Siddhartha Forest was not what I would have chosen, given the work that needed doing and other problematic things in the situation like a difficult guest who was refusing to leave. Rachael was also not happy about it – she didn't want to move yet again – but eventually agreed to do so when she was able to choose her new room. Siddhartha Forest was what was available, and I heard the place calling to me as Buddha Garden seemed to be saying it was time for me to leave.

As I moved I realized that as well as giving up the vision of Buddha Garden I was also giving up the vision of ever living in a community. It seemed that all my life I had been looking for a sense of belonging and never really found it. I had the feeling that I had to be on my own -- that there wasn't a community for me anywhere. I made the move not knowing why I was in Auroville or what I was really meant to be doing. All I could see was the next step which was to go to Siddhartha Forest, make a home for myself and Rachael and spend more time on my writing and painting which would hopefully help me understand the difficult events of the previous year.

I determined that I would nurture the satisfying relationships I did have, however unlike 'what I want' they seemed to be. That day-by-day I would continue trying to see how my outer world was a mirror for the inner, and vice versa, and what this meant for me.

Be
Where you are

How I Grew With My Garden

Create
A place of transformation

Be with those
Who enable the
Alchemy within.

******

I wish I could say that during my six months in Siddhartha Forest I wrote my book and in doing so obtained the clarity I wanted. That I had breakthroughs on an internal level that enabled me to understand what was going on in Buddha Garden, so I could plan for the future. Breakthroughs that provided me with an equanimity which enabled me to go back to Buddha Garden feeling positive knowing that I could accept whatever life chose to give me. An equanimity that enabled me to accept both the negative and the positive with equal balance. Breakthroughs that gave me a knowing of the Divine or whatever it was that enabled my inner flame to burn and not be extinguished during the darkest of times.

I wish.

******

In the beginning I enjoyed the extra time I had for myself. To be able to get up every morning and know that I could do whatever I wanted. That it wasn't my responsibility to go out into the garden. That I didn't need to be the prime mover any more. That I could have a leisurely breakfast with Rachael and then do whatever I liked. For some time I felt too tired to do anything except lie around and read – fortunately my friend had sent me a stack of books for Christmas and I also spent a lot of time in the Auroville library.

I felt like I was drifting. That I had gone to a place beyond words. I didn't know what to do; my normal organizing skills seemed to have deserted me. I thought I would love having all the extra time to write and paint, but I didn't feel like doing anything. I seemed to drift around in a fog, this lasting from the winter solstice to the New Year which seemed to bring in changes but which were very hard to put into words.

WHAT I DO NOW

Look deeply with intensity and focus
Look softly allowing revelation to show itself

Love myself dreaming.

In such a situation it didn't surprise me that my painful feelings of loss surfaced yet again and I started to feel very depressed and also got quite sick. Fortunately this did not overwhelm me in the way that it had done previously and I took this as a sign that maybe things were improving. My usually decisive nature seemed to have deserted me and I found myself taking a long time to decide about small things. One morning it took me half an hour to decide whether to go to Buddha Garden to fetch the vegetables or to have a drink first. Gradually I started to paint and write again but it was very sporadic. My diary entries of the time are also patchy and uninformative which could be revelatory of how alienated I continued to feel from most things and most people.

******

Fortunately there were still some practical things to do which were not too time-consuming and included making our own vegetable garden and dealing with with the gardener who had been asked to leave as the project money that supported him had ended. This was a difficult task as not unnaturally the gardener was angry at losing his job and although we gave him a good bonus and reference and tried to explain about why the there was no money, he continued to cause problems. Several times he pulled down the fence and once he started a fire which burnt a patch of the forest. In many ways it seemed things had not changed but with it not being my place and with two of us to sort things out it wasn't as bad as it could have been.

Once the time of languor had passed much of my time was spent on the research for the Farm Assessment process. I had made a start on it while in Buddha Garden but had found I couldn't get on with the work when I was feeling so exhausted. I was once a professional market researcher and, much to my surprise I found that, like riding a bicycle, there were skills that I had not forgotten. Despite the late start, the work was completed more or less on time and although I found it interesting and to some extent enjoyable, I knew that my heart was now elsewhere in other sorts of work.

When the results of the Farm Assessment were gathered, I was very heartened to find that the soil in Buddha Garden vegetable garden was the best of all the farms in Auroville. Soil samples from the rest of Buddha Garden showed the soil to be, if anything, worse than other farms. When I came to Buddha Garden I had wanted to heal a piece of the earth and to some extent this has happened. There was no resting on our laurels, however, as although the soil was better than elsewhere in Auroville, the nitrogen content was still below generally accepted minimum levels needed for optimum plant growth. It showed that we can make a difference, that we can bring fertility to the soil if we are willing to put in the necessary consistent work………..but that the hard work needed to continue.

******

I continued to go to Buddha Garden regularly to collect vegetables and at such times I talked a lot to John about what he was doing. I saw how he concentrated on producing vegetables - which he was doing very successfully – but that the volunteers were less involved with the whole process. John and his worker tended to do most of the work with volunteers doing odd jobs as they arose. I had thought that I would find it difficult to let go of the work completely and had arranged with John that I would come and work some mornings if I felt like it. I never did.

Nevertheless, I continued to think about whether I should return to Buddha Garden or not, with thoughts going up and down and round and round in myself like a fairground ride. I did all the usual things – I wrote about it, talked about it and painted but still couldn't come to any decision.

One day a friend of mine from the Health Centre phoned and asked me if I had work for a young man who had only one arm. He explained at some length how this individual had been doing garden work for some time, so even with his disability he could do a good job. The man was quite young – only 16 or so – but came from a poor family where he was the only one capable of earning money so he desperately needed a job. I explained that there was no work in Buddha Garden but as I did so I wondered how many other young people there were who would like such a job – especially perhaps if it also included learning a skill while at the same time earning money.

Looking back, it's difficult to tell exactly how the idea of the apprenticeship programme came into existence. My friend's phone call sparked off the idea when I was thinking about what I needed in Buddha Garden in terms of long-term help. How I also wanted Buddha Garden to be a place where people came to learn and wanted to involve the volunteers both in the work and in learning. It was from this that the idea of a 'community of learners' and the 'Learning on the Land' programme was conceptualized.

My idea was that there would be a number of apprentices who would, with the volunteers, carry out the practical work on the land together from 6.30 – 9.00am each day as well as doing the regular afternoon and weekend jobs on a rota basis. There would be an education session from 10.00 – 12.00 which would include acquiring basic skills such as language, maths and computing together with opportunities to explore and expand their horizons on any topics that interested them. 'Life skills' would also be taught together with meditation, reflection and discussion about the spiritual basis of life.

An important aspect of the programme would be the opportunity it would provide for apprentices and volunteers to learn from each other. Volunteers would be asked to do an introductory session about themselves and, if they would like to, share any passions or skills that they had. Apprentices would help the volunteers with the practical work as well as offer an insight into the local culture – if that seemed to be appropriate.

******

It was at this time that Derek came to stay in Siddhartha Forest while working as a volunteer in Buddha Garden. He was very interested in the apprenticeship programme and it was my talking with him that enabled me to clarify a lot of my ideas. I was delighted when he said that he would like to be a part of it. Here at last was someone who shared the vision and with whom I felt I could work and who wanted to come to Buddha Garden to work with me. He was also interested in writing a book about his experiences in his community in Canada so that all fitted as well.

I talked with several people in Auroville about the project and had some very positive replies. I also talked with several Tamil friends of mine, who might have known of possible students. Although they were very enthusiastic one friend pointed out that such a programme was likely to be viewed with some mystification by the local people. The idea that one could do a 'low status' job like farming and still have some education, especially with computers, was outside most peoples' experience. He told me he had had some problems trying to explain the concept to people that he knew. Nevertheless he thought it was a marvelous idea and suggested that I start with a few people who wanted to participate. Once everyone could see and then understand the programme he thought I would be heavily over subscribed for the next intake.

Almost immediately I had several people came to see me about the possibility of participating and eventually there were nine potential apprentices waiting for the project to start.

******

As the six-month deadline came into view John was adamant that he wanted to leave. It seemed as if I was going to go back but I still felt ambivalent about it. It seemed that even with the new programme things were still very much as they had been when I left. I would be going back to run everything on my own. It was true I would have the help of the apprentices but I would also have more responsibilities and with the education programme to organize, even more to do.

I was also concerned that during the months away I had not reached any real clarity about my situation as I had hoped to do. I had wanted to understand the undermining and other things that happened to me in the previous year, but I was no clearer about it than when I came. Similarly as to whether I should stay in Auroville or not, I was not definite about that either. I felt I was moving towards this new project with all this untransformed material and I wondered what the effect of this would be. I had started Buddha Garden and it didn't turn out as I had hoped, so here I was starting another project without understanding why the previous one didn't work. Was this just another diversion from myself and my pain which seemed so immoveable? Would I end up in exactly the same place a few years on when this project had run its course?

A conversation in one of the Farm Group meetings made me think about why things hadn't fundamentally changed in Buddha Garden.

ME: '*I'm going to be moving back to Buddha Garden at the beginning of July.*'
FARM GROUP MEMBER: '*But we don't think you have ever left!*'

Even Derek said that when he was working in Buddha Garden he felt very much that I was still there.

Perhaps I hadn't let go of Buddha Garden as I should have done. Because I had perhaps never really left, the space for change hadn't been created and change hadn't happened. Derek suggested that maybe I should have left Auroville completely. He had left his Canadian community to come to Auroville and apparently there had been huge changes while he had been away. With Rachael still at school in Auroville, leaving completely hadn't been an option and although I had looked long and hard for a house farther away from Buddha Garden, it was the house in Siddhartha Forest that had presented itself to me. Had I wasted this time? I wished that I had somehow written more or somehow sorted out more things inside myself. In many ways, moving inexorably back to Buddha Garden, I felt more confused than I did when I left.

******

In the two hot months before I was due to return to Buddha Garden I decided to get completely removed from Siddhartha Forest, especially as I could do so with Rachael going to the UK for a holiday. I went to stay in several houses vacated by friends leaving Auroville where I had terrific urges to write but no inspiration. I wanted to engage with the act of putting words on paper, but ridiculously had no idea of what those words might be. I wanted to express something, but what it was eluded me. I did, however, feel strongly pulled with the new project and ended up writing about it and several other things about Buddha Garden for the web site.

Two weeks before I was due to move back, I started working in the mornings again. Every now and then I would have moments of great joy at the thought of returning. As I worked I felt more energised but was aware, of course, with the new programme and the extra work that entailed, the challenge was going to be about how to keep that energy level. At times I also felt very grey and the thought of going back there on my own again felt very bleak.

A few days before moving I had a dream which seemed to go with me. It was about the French underground where I traveled without bags or maps trying to find my daughter. I think I was being asked to examine the knowledge that I really needed, which according to the dream was internal rather than external and could not be grasped in a linear fashion. I was aware that the knowledge was there for anyone who had cultivated the sensitivity to see and sense it. So perhaps the fact that I didn't understand what had happened in the previous year didn't matter as much as I thought it did. I didn't need to sit and think so much as be extra aware and sensitive to events so that understanding could arise.

As a result I felt better despite my not having found the understanding and clarity as I had hoped. What I had to do was not lose sight of the fact that I didn't understand, and thereby cultivate the necessary conditions under which understanding and awareness could arise. This meant that I had to have enough time for myself which would probably mean leaving Buddha Garden for short periods at regular intervals.

******

At the beginning of July, John and I exchanged houses and I moved back to Buddha Garden while he went to Siddhartha Forest. It was, as usual, a very intense time especially as I was fitting myself into the much smaller space of what used to be my art room. The lower room was now going to be used as the education room for the apprenticeship programme. I put a lot of my things into the new store room and distributed my books between the education room and the volunteer room, but even so, it seemed a small space for everything that I needed. Rachael went back to her old room, the one on top of the store room.

The next few weeks were extremely demanding; I felt as if I had to run at top speed just to stay in the same place. Taking over the running of the farm was not so difficult although I was upset to see that in the week before I arrived, a group of cows had got into the garden and eaten all the maize which greatly reduced our sales in the following weeks. There was also the education programme for the apprentices to be established which meant that after the early morning work in the farm I spent most of the rest of the morning doing various sorts of teaching, or organising others to do so. I was also very aware that I had to raise money to pay for this as, although I had managed to raise some money it would not last very long and it was obvious that the farm would not be able to pay for the programme. A new group of volunteers arrived soon after I moved in, several of them students needing help with their research projects. It was an extremely intense time when a timeless quality infused long periods of the day until I saw with surprise that it was sunset once again.

Given that inspiration for all my other books has arisen during periods of intense activity, I suppose I shouldn't have been surprised when the idea for this book came at such a time. I had been waiting and hoping for inspiration for so long. I was mystified. Why did it come now when I had so much else to do? How was I going to find time to write this book? How was I going to find the time to do that, and focus on my inner process and meditate enough? How was I going to make sure that I didn't get burnt out again when I had a greatly increased work load and was still on my own?

****

Morning work in the garden took on a new dimension with eight eager young men wanting to help. There was considerable variation in how much experience they had of work on the land but being local people they were used to the climate, the crops we were growing and the tools – unlike the volunteers. They learnt very quickly and began to pick up the rhythms of the practical work. With this and the help of the volunteers the work flowed easily and I was often pleasantly surprised at just how much we managed to do. Derek also joined us in Buddha Garden, and after a few weeks Arjunan also came back, having just returned from Arcosanti with his Japanese fiancé.

At first it was clear that the apprentices felt that they had nothing to share with the volunteers, but as time passed this changed. An important step was when one volunteer came requesting that the apprentices help her interview local farmers for her research   The apprentices found two farmers willing to be interviewed and then went with the volunteer to translate what the farmer said. They all came back feeling very pleased with themselves and it was obvious that everyone had learnt something.
I felt that I had to try and clear a space for my own writing which meant tackling a backlog of regular jobs that had built up during the move. I felt strongly that I needed to divest myself of some of this work and over the next few weeks managed to do this, finding others to take these jobs. Nevertheless I continued to feel very pressurised with many demands on my attention, sometimes finding it more or less impossible to sit quietly at a job for any period of time. Often I felt pulverized with so much to do and so many people needing something from me. It felt like having a demanding young baby, which in a sense with this new project, was what I had.

Despite the demands of the situation there was a feeling of rightness about it that I hadn't experienced for a very long time. I had started to write my diary and paint, to do those things that were an important expression of my inner life. I felt as if I were back in my process, the important inner process where the deeper river of my inner self flowed.

******

This tenuous equilibrium was shattered when I was woken by a very distressed Rachael at 2.00am one morning. She asked me to come quickly to her room as she had had two intruders there. She had woken up and noticed that her door was open which immediately alerted her as she always closed the door before going to bed. She saw something black against the white wall and thought it was our black dog until she saw an arm reach forward as the person crawled across the floor. She sat up very quickly and this person and his accomplice outside ran away down the steps. That was when she phoned me.

Naturally she was very frightened and upset and we spent the rest of the night in my bed discussing whether it had been a dream. Later we cleared her room with incense and she took one of the dogs into her room at night to feel safer.

So once again we were feeling very violated and quite numb. With all the intensity of the last month and the seemingly ever increasing demands on my energy it was my way of coping. How was it that ideas for my writing were still continuing to flow? It was as if I were living in two different and unconnected worlds.

******

At the end of the first month, with the move completed and the apprentices established, we decided to have a meditation to celebrate. The apprentices worked very hard, making a beautiful unity symbol and generally decorating the place to look very lovely with flowers and incense and candles. We held the meditation in the stone circle and spent several days cutting the grass, with Derek creating a picture of a hawk in small stones in an inner circle in the middle. We sang and chanted as the sun set and as it got darker the flickering oil lamps made the hawk look as if it were flying. That night I had a dream.

MEDITATION DREAM

A tree alone
Ancient

Leaves limply hanging
Bedraggled

Tree fruits softly cobweb
Covered

Next morning a spider sat in my hair.
The one that - years ago - sewed up
My broken heart.

I have always felt a special affinity with spiders. When my partner died and I felt as if the person who had murdered him had put a sword through my heart, over the weeks and months that followed, in my imagination it was a spider who came and sewed it up. In this dream I felt that the spiders had a similar role and were somehow helping the tree to put something old away to make way for something new.

****

As if all the changes over the previous months had not been enough, Rachael then decided that she wanted to return to the UK so that she could do her secondary schooling there. She started talking about it in mid-August. Ten days later, in time for the start of the new school year in the UK, she left to go and live with her half brother and his partner and baby. It was a difficult decision for her as she had spent most of her life in Auroville and had a wonderful group of friends, but she also wanted the sort of education that isn't available here. I wanted her to stay, but once she was clear that this was the right decision for her, I obviously couldn't stand in her way.

It was a whirlwind time of change which seemed to have hit so suddenly out of the blue.

Then a few days before she was due to leave someone came into her room, while she was asleep, and stole her laptop computer and speakers. Someone who knew what they were doing as they took not only the computer but unhitched all the electrical connectors. Someone must have known, someone must have been watching her going-away party with all her friends and known that she would be deeply asleep. It was partly her fault as she hadn't locked the computer desk, but even so it was a horrible thing to happen just days before she was due to leave.

I cried and cried. How I hated not being able to feel safe and having to lock all my things up like Fort Knox. I had poured money into this place along with my heart and soul and it seemed all the time that people would come and take whatever they could. This felt so much like another inside job, someone who knew exactly where the computer was and how to unhitch it, and maybe also that Rachael would be deeply asleep because of the party.

I plumbed to a depth of despair I had never reached before.

******

Two days later, very early in the morning I said goodbye to Rachael at Chennai airport. A few days later I started moving my things to what used to be her room over the store room. This made an extra room for the apprenticeship programme – it is now the quiet room where we do art and sometimes meditate.

Later I painted a picture of an empty woman – which was much how I felt after the burglary and with Rachael gone. I looked at the pictures of Emma and Rachael. I thought how I hadn't seen Emma for over a year and how I was missing Rachael, although it seemed that she had jumped into her new life and wasn't missing me.

Then I saw how my prayers for time and space to write had been answered.

I am adrift.

A vast emptiness with
In a barren space.

Those once close
Are now distant,
Or unreachable.

Warm intimacy supplanted
By lonely bleakness.

A blank nothingness.

The answer to my prayer
For time and space to write

PART FIVE

REGENERATION

WEAVING THE WEB BEING WOVEN

Now the book is written and the point has been reached where the book is finished although the process it describes is not.

Looking at the garden I can see and feel the outer transformation that has taken place. I feel how in the process of that transformation I have accessed that deeper river within me and to some extent have slowly become more at one with it. Farming has taught me, perhaps more than any other work, that to create is always to co-create, sometimes with forces that are beyond control and always with the rhythms of the seasons.

Once I would weave webs of candy floss
Carefully knotting the delicate sugar threads
Into fabulous lacy concoctions
Their cloying sweetness
Glittering pinkly in the sun

And those I caught in such webs
Loved me for my sweet goodness.

Once I would weave webs of spun steel
Twisting and turning the thin hard metal
Into fantastic shapes and ethereal constructions
Their clever intricacies, dazzling
The minds of all who saw.

And those I caught in such webs
Loved me for my intelligent creativity.

Once I would weave webs of lightning and fireworks
Cacophony of exploding sound and light, woven
Into a dancing kaleidoscope of radiance
In a grey sky.

And those I caught in such webs
Loved me for my ardent energy.

Now I have no more webs to weave,
For I am the web being woven.

There are still many things, however, which I do not feel that I understand or accept. I still find it very hard to carry out this work alone and the dynamics within the situation still seem to put me at the centre in the role of the motivator and anchor. So far my efforts to change this have come to nothing, something that concerns me as I do not feel I am personally very sustainable working like this. I wonder how much longer I can carry on without getting tired and burnt out again. Nor am I any clearer as to how I might find or attract someone who would come to work with me and hold this vision with me on a permanent basis.

Reflecting on these issues does not provide me with any answers although it enables me to constantly make sure that I am using the energies that are available in the best way possible. Maybe the answer to these dilemmas will be solved by changing something within me on a different level of my being. I continue to write and paint as part of expressing my internal process and perhaps eventually this will enable me to penetrate this mystery.

******

Last month three of the apprentices came to live here in Buddha Garden. I am not sure whether this is going to be successful as I was concerned that if they came to live in Auroville they might, while not becoming completely integrated in Auroville, also find it difficult to return to village life when the course is finished. I was also concerned that it might split the group with the resident apprentices feeling differently about the project than those who were non-resident. We talked about this at some length and eventually we decided that we would try it for one month.

So far it seems to be working very well. From time-to-time we have had to decide what we are going to do about things like drinking alcohol and having parties and in deciding about these things the whole group of apprentices has been involved. Most of the non-resident apprentices have stayed the night from time-to-time and as a result they all feel the same sense of integration with the place.

Thus starts another cycle of growth both for Buddha Garden and for me. I feel this new direction is like a sucker on a banana bush, a new and strong shoot growing directly from the roots of the original plant – something new arising from the roots of the old idea of Buddha Garden. After feeling as if I were under siege from the local people it is very healing for me to be with this group of young men in such a positive way. Together we will continue to transform the outer landscape of Buddha Garden and let this be the roots for the process of transformation within.

INVOCATION

*I would like to live closely
With You and you both.
Creating a vibrant joy as we*

Dance our truth.

*Together I would like us to
Engage with the earth that
Sustains and supports us.*

*Making the ground from
Which we can stretch to
Express our being.*

Singing our heart songs.

*Making a nest for our children
From which they can fly, high
And free on strong wings.*

******

ABOUT AUROVILLE

Auroville draws its inspiration from the work of the Indian spiritual visionary Sri Aurobindo and was founded in 1968 by his spiritual collaborator known as the Mother. Both Sri Aurobindo and the Mother had expressed in their earliest writings the necessity of starting, at some point, a collective experiment - ideally in the form of a city - to create a bridgehead for a new consciousness which was seeking to manifest in the world. The Ashram, formally created in Pondicherry in 1926, was a first attempt in that direction. Here, in 1964, the idea of Auroville was first conceived:

'Auroville wants to be a universal town where men and women of all countries are able to live in peace and progressive harmony, above all creeds, all politics and all nationalities. The Purpose of Auroville is to realise human unity.'

The name 'Auroville' was given in homage to Sri Aurobindo, while also having the most appropriate meaning, 'City of Dawn'.

In an inauguration ceremony which took place on February 28th 1968 the Charter of Auroville, written by the Mother was first heard. For me it is still the most succinct and inspiring description of the ideals on which Auroville is based.

1. Auroville belongs to nobody in particular. Auroville belongs to humanity as a whole. But to live in Auroville one must be a willing servitor of the Divine Consciousness.
2. Auroville will be a place of unending education. Of constant progress and a youth that never ages.
3. Auroville wants to be the bridge between the past and the future. Taking advantage of discoveries from without and from within. Auroville will boldly spring towards future realisations.
4. Auroville will be a site of material and spiritual researches for a living embodiment of an actual Human Unity.

Auroville is now an emerging international township of over 1,500 people from India and more than 30 other nations who pursue a very wide range of practical activities necessary for its upkeep and development. These include village development, education, land restoration, business, research into renewable energy and experimental construction techniques, health care and varied cultural activities. Whatever the outer activity and material achievements, however, the main aim is inner change. For without an inner change in consciousness no permanent outer change is possible. All practical activities are not merely tasks which are necessary for the functioning of the township, but opportunities for bringing consciousness into matter and with it the possibility for a new way of being to emerge.

For further details go to www.auroville.org

Printed in Great Britain by
Amazon.co.uk, Ltd.,
Marston Gate.